Marx and Philosophy of Culture

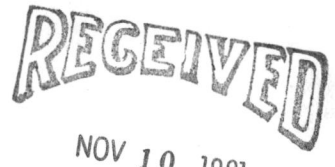

NOV 10 1981

FLORIDA BOARD OF REGENTS
STATE UNIVERSITY SYSTEM
OFFICE OF THE CHANCELLOR

University of Florida Monographs

Humanities Number 50

Marx and Philosophy of Culture

Robert D'Amico

A University of Florida Book

University Presses of Florida
Gainesville

EDITORIAL COMMITTEE

Humanities Monographs

RAYMOND GAY-CROSIER, *Chairman*
Professor of Romance Languages and
  Literature

ELLEN HARING
Professor of Philosophy

MILDRED A. HILL-LUBIN
Associate Professor of English and
  Graduate School Liaison

HELGA KRAFT
Associate Professor of Germanic and
  Slavic Languages and Literature

GARETH L. SCHMELING
Professor of Classics

ROBERT WESTIN
Associate Professor of Art

Library of Congress Cataloging in Publication Data

D'Amico, Robert.
  Marx and philosophy of culture.

  (University of Florida monographs: Humanities; no. 50)
  "A University of Florida book."
  Bibliography: p.
  Includes index.
  1. Marx, Karl, 1818–1883. 2. Culture—Philosophy.
3. Civilization—Philosophy. 4. Work.
5. Economics. 6. Act (Philosophy) I. Title.
II. Series: Florida. University, Gainesville.
University of Florida monographs: Humanities; no. 50.
B3305.M74D33   335.4′01   80-24405
ISBN 0-8130-0689-9

University Presses of Florida is the central agency for scholarly publishing of the State of Florida's university system. Its offices are located at 15 NW 15th Street, Gainesville, FL 32603. Works published by University Presses of Florida are evaluated and selected for publication by a faculty editorial committee of any one of Florida's nine public universities: Florida A&M University (Tallahassee), Florida Atlantic University (Boca Raton), Florida International University (Miami), Florida State University (Tallahassee), University of Central Florida (Orlando), University of Florida (Gainesville), University of North Florida (Jacksonville), University of South Florida (Tampa), University of West Florida (Pensacola).

COPYRIGHT © 1981 BY THE BOARD OF REGENTS OF THE
STATE OF FLORIDA

PRINTED IN U.S.A.

Preface

My interest in investigating what Marx had to contribute concerning the relationship between culture and the economy arose as a result of both theoretical and practical concerns. In the theory I had been struck by the discrepancy between the rich and complex nature of Marx's actual writings and the poor schematic representation of his position in the general literature. It seemed to me that both in criticisms of Marx and in the simplified principles of orthodox Marxism, the philosophically interesting issues were ignored and problems in Marx's terminology were avoided. By turning to the concept of culture one could confront the appeal to purely economic explanations as a symptom of this general theoretical reduction of Marx's work. Practically, in a similar fashion, I had noted the shift in leftist politics from orthodox analysis of economic crises to different forms of cultural criticism using such themes as the family, consumption, morality, and sexuality, which are not dealt with in Marx's writings. The connection was obviously that a general understanding of Marx's theory should respond to the political significance of culture in modern capitalism.

It is very difficult to claim originality in interpreting Marx in view of the enormous literature that now exists on his work. Instead of attempting a dramatic change in the view of Marx, I have simply argued that the concept of labor, for better or worse, is philosophically central to Marx's work. Marx uses the term *labor* in a special way, and therefore I have used examples from his own analyses as well as from contemporary theoreticians to bring out its role in his overall theory. Though the contemporary theoreticians I have chosen are probably not familiar to Anglo-American philosophy, I believe that the basic issues will be familiar to anyone interested in philosophy of the social sciences or philosophy of action.

I could not have begun this work without the opportunity to attend lectures on Hegel and Marx and study with Mitchel Franklin, now professor emeritus of philosophy and law at the State University of New York at Buffalo. I owe a special thanks to Professor Paul Piccone and the associate editors of the journal *Telos*; I covered some of the issues in this study in an article entitled "Desire and the Commodity-Form" in its Spring 1978 issue. Hugh Silverman, Greg Ulmer, and Patti Hartz read various versions of this manuscript and offered valuable criticisms and encouragement. Finally during the time that I thought about and tried to write about these issues, Susan Armstrong was there, and this work is some small recognition of her support.

Contents

1. Marx's Concept of Labor — 1
2. The Economic and the Symbolic in Culture — 16
3. Objects and Utility — 44
4. The Production of Desire — 58
5. Ideology and Knowledge in Marx — 75
Notes — 95
Bibliography — 101
Index — 107

There is no document of civilization which is not
at the same time a document of barbarism.
Walter Benjamin

1. Marx's Concept of Labor

To understand what Marx means by the term superstructure and how that metaphor encompasses the culture of a society, one must come to terms with the concept of labor. Though there could be little disagreement that labor is central to the whole of Marx's social analyses, there is still little agreement on precisely what Marx meant by the term. What kind of explanation does the concept of labor provide for the formation of society and culture? Marx was always loose in his use of fundamental concepts and relegated clarification of his terms to extremely condensed philosophical disgressions. Only in notebooks and self-clarifying exercises did Marx try to fix a fundamental vocabulary. These works, which were not meant for publication, have only recently been used in the study of Marx's thought. However, they are now invaluable to gaining an overall view of Marx's development and as a guide for interpreting the published material. In the case of the term *labor* we find a wealth of theoretical articulation in the early notebooks of 1844, *The Economic and Philosophic Manuscripts* (volume 5 of the *Collected Works*, referred to as the *Paris Manuscripts*), and in the later series of notebooks that Marx used for the preparation of *Capital*, now referred to as the *Grundrisse*. From these texts and their theoretical and philosophical themes, the role of the concept of labor in Marx can be genetically reconstructed.

Marx is still considered by most historians of ideas as an economic determinist. The basis of all society is economic activity; therefore, culture is a mere effect or at best a rationalization of economic pursuits. If Marx had held such a view, it would at least have put him into basic agreement with the classical political economists. Adam Smith's *The Wealth of Nations* presents just such a picture of civilization. The human propensity to "truck and barter" is placed at the foundation of all social life, and the advance of modern civilization is seen to rest on the extension of the division of labor. Smith's position derived in large part from the Enlightenment reaction to the strictures of feudal social structures. Against the "dark ages" Smith and others offered a defense and rehabilitation of the market and merchant as civilizing forces. In Bernard Mandeville's *The Fable of the Bees* (1791), for example, we find the argument that the civilizing process and the public benefits of wealth proceed not from Christian virtues but from the baser instincts of self-interest. In other words, not traditional morality but precisely its opposite, the motivations of greed, avarice, and self-interest, sustain and support the social order. All that Marx brought to this analysis, we are told, was an acute awareness of the abuses inherent in the rule of the economy over society. However, it is assumed that the term *economic* remains continuous between Marx and the tradition of political economy and that Marx shared the same fundamental account of social life.

In the following presentation of how Marx formulated and developed the concept of labor as essential human activity, I want to suggest another view. Let us assume that Marx designed his main concepts against the economic determinism and utilitarianism of *Homo economicus*. If there is a discontinuity between Marx and political economy, it suggests that Marx also did not embrace the reduction of culture to its economic function nor the ontological division between culture and the economy that is assumed by a doctrine of economic determinism.

For Marx, labor is a philosophical rather than an economic concept. Marx, of course, criticized the enterprise of metaphysics but did not reject the necessity for theoretical reflection on the limits and presuppositions of knowledge. Marx's aim was not absolute truth but the expression of what is universal in human history. Therefore, to say that labor is a philosophical concept in Marx means precisely that labor is part of a fundamental theory of human activity or ontology of social life. Marx constructed this theory systematically as part of his historical work. It is this theory of human activity that is found mostly in notes, digressions, and Marx's unpublished writings. Such a theory of human action is the ground of Marx's research and provides a critique of both the utilitarian model of action and the determinism of traditional political economy. Finally, if labor is just such a synthetic concept in Marx, then the relation between culture and superstructure must be reconsidered. The traditional interpretation of Marx reduces all culture to the hidden hand of economic gain. At most culture serves to conceal the real processes of social life from those who suffer under its inexorable laws. If Marx, on the other hand, rejected the model of a determining economic structure, then culture is not simply the functional extension of production or a veil over the baser instinct of monetary hunger. Marx's theory of human activity and concept of labor treats *Homo economicus* as a distortion and corruption of human life. Labor is more than utility in Marx, and therefore culture is not simply an illusion. Marx did not hold that the economy is the sole determination of human activity; on the contrary, it is the mode of life activity that determines the place of the economy in society.

The first step, therefore, in explaining the connection between culture and superstructure is a clarification of this theory of human activity in Marx. Marx's most important formulations of labor as a philosophical concept are found in the *Paris Manuscripts* of 1844–45. These are the notebooks that the young Marx composed in Paris under the influence of French utopian socialism and a first reading of political economy. In a very speculative and obscure style Marx attempts a synthesis of the concepts of Hegelian idealism and social analysis. The most successful aspect of this failed work is Marx's theory of human labor as objectification. Mankind, for Marx, makes itself in the act of making its world. This activity is called objectification, and in its essential form it is labor. The power of labor or objectification distinguishes humanity from nature by constituting for itself a surrounding world, a world of objectivities. It is this world of human objects that in turn forms and conditions humanity itself. Marx calls this relationship between the subject and object of labor an act of self-objectification. The human subject does not confront a world of dead matter; rather it confronts a human order, a realm of meaning and purpose embedded in objectivities. Objectification, as the product of human action, is the embodiment of human motivation, purpose, and ends. Precisely because meaning is brought to the material world by activity, the world in turn can act upon and condition the humanity that dwells within it. Labor, for Marx, is a self-objectification in which the object is subjected to human purpose but the subject objectified in the world of objects is transformed by such action. It is the whole activity of labor that Marx calls purposive activity: "The product of labour is labour which has been embodied in an object, which has become material; it is the *objectification* of labour. Labour's realization is its objectification."[1]

Marx calls this activity the essence of man. Labor or purposive activity is the species-being of man. The term *species-being* means that labor is both the universal, the distinctly human in reality, and that which necessitates the social rather than natural life of humanity. "The productive life is the life of the species, it is life-engendering life. The whole character of a species—its species-character—is contained in the character of its life activity; and free, conscious activity in man's species-character."[2]

But labor as life activity, as the free manifestation and enjoyment of life, remains an unrealized potential as long as the product exists in the form of private property. The thrust of the *Paris Manuscripts* is to attack the reduction of human production or self-objectification to the act of possession, accumulation of wealth, and monetary gain. "Private property has made us so stupid and one-sided that an object is only *ours* when we have it—when it exists for us as capital, or when it is directly possessed, eaten, drunk, worn, inhabited, etc.—in short, when it is *used* by us. Although private property itself again conceives all these direct realizations of possession only as *means of life*, . . . the life which they serve as means is the *life of private property*."[3]

Within these historically imposed limits, labor as life activity turns into its opposite, namely the drudgery, domination, and denial of life demanded by wage labor. Therefore Marx clearly argues that labor as our essential activity is destroyed precisely when it is manifested only as an economic, calculating action of self-interest. "Each of us sees in his product only the objectification of his *own* selfish need, and therefore in the product of the other the objectification of a *different* selfish need, independent of him and alien to him."[4]

Marx's arguments show that political economy, in its defense of private property, was contradicted by both human essence and the possible full realization of human life. In opposition Marx refers not to economic factors but to a wider philosophical concept of labor in life. Marx praises Hegel for having approached social life as the objectification of human intentions and history as the struggle over the alienation of that activity through its appropriation. In doing this Marx shows clearly that the vocabulary in which he conceives of the labor process is entirely philosophical and not restricted to the realm of economy. "The outstanding achievement of Hegel's *Phenomenology* and its final outcome, the dialectic of negativity as the moving and generating principle, is then first that Hegel conceives the self-creation of man as a process, conceives objectification as the loss of the object, as alienation and as transcendence of this alienation: that he grasps the essence of *labour* and comprehends objective man—true, because real man—as the outcome of man's *own labour*."[5]

The concept of the human world as that which is made by man himself predates Hegel. In Giambattista Vico we find a very early text distinguishing between nature and culture through the power of humanity to make its world and thus be conditioned by its own actions. "But in the night of thick darkness enveloping the earliest antiquity, so remote from ourselves, there remains the eternal and never failing light of a truth beyond all question: that the world of civil society has certainly been made by men, and that its principles are therefore to be found within the modifications of our own human mind. Whoever reflects on this cannot but marvel that the philosophers should have bent all their energies to the study of the world of nature, which, since God made it, he alone knows; and that they should have neglected the study of the world of nations, or civil world, which, since men had made it, men could come to know."[6]

Hegel went further than any other thinker, however, in fully presenting a theory of history on the basis of self-production. In the Hegelian system, Spirit (*Geist*) manifests itself, throughout history, in objectifications, externalizations, and alienations that represent forms of consciousness. Spirit comes to understand itself through the history of these objectifications. Spirit is ultimately the reason inherent in history as a teleological process. Hegel calls objectification a power of negativity because the objectifications of Spirit transform and therefore negate what is given in reality. Human labor is just such a manifestation of the power of Spirit. Labor modifies its world and thereby allows man to know it and free itself from the bonds of natural necessity. "Man with his necessities sustains a practical relation to external nature and in making it satisfy his desires and using it up mediates it through labor. Natural objects are powerful and offer forms of resistance. In order to subdue them, man introduces other natural agents that turn Nature against itself and invents a tool [*Werkzeuge*] toward this end. These human conventions belong to Spirit and therefore a tool is held in higher esteem than a mere natural object."[7]

Hegel stresses two aspects of the role of labor as objectification. First, labor is defined as that which mediates the world. By the term mediation Hegel means that the human world becomes transformed (mediated) by activity and purpose and therefore is no longer a world of natural objects. Culture or Spirit is precisely the objectification of this teleology or mediation. Second, practical activity, by giving meaning to its world, creates a "second nature" which conditions humanity. Since what is conditioning humanity is the externalization of its own purposive activity, it is conditioned by its own product and not an external, natural object. For that reason Hegel calls it a "second" or constituted nature. For example, law and morality condition and form human beings through a process of cultivation (*Bildungsweise*) or civilizing influence. Humanity is realizing itself through objectifications of its own activity. "For law is the objectivity of Spirit; it is will in its true form. . . . an Athenian citizen did what was required of him, as it were from instinct. But if I reflect on the object of my activity, I must have the consciousness that my will counts. Morality, however, is this duty, the substantial law, the second nature, as it has been rightly called; for the first nature of man is his immediate, animalic existence."[8]

Therefore the process of objectification is characterized by consciousness and mediation and is wholly distinct from the determinism of the natural world. The idea of second nature is related then to what Marx describes as the socialization or civilization of humanity through the products of its own hands. But Marx saw a profound limitation in Hegel's account of labor. In Hegel labor is only a manifestation of Spirit, and Spirit is ultimately a principle of reason meant to transcend the limits of the human world. When Marx summarized his attitude to Hegel's viewpoint, he called it abstract and therefore philosophical in the traditional sense. "Let us provisionally say this much in advance: Hegel's standpoint is that of modern political economy. He grasps *labour* as the *essence* of man—as man's essence which stands the test: he sees only the positive, not the negative side of labour. Labour is *man's coming-to-be himself* within *alienation*, or as *alienated* man. The only labour which Hegel knows and recognizes is *abstractly mental* labor."[9]

Marx begins by noting that both Hegel and the political economists recognized the central importance of labor in society. But Hegel only saw labor in its abstract, intellectual form. For Hegel, Marx argues, the categories of negativity and mediation are ultimately devoid of social meaning, for they are meant to point thought beyond all material reality. Therefore, labor in Hegel is simply a metaphor for the power of thought to negate and transform its world. Labor in the material world is a shadow of its spiritual significance and serves as a vessel for the movement of Spirit. But in Marx the world is the irreducible and finite reality for all thought. History cannot be transcended by philosophical contemplation nor can the human mind have access to absolute knowledge. Human history, for Marx, remains bound to a finite material world which is knowable only as the objectification of human action.

Therefore when Marx says that Hegel does not understand the negative side of labor, he means specifically that Hegel does not see the social and historical limits placed on human labor. For Hegel labor is just another objectification of thought that will culminate in philosophical transcendence. Since Hegel constructs his theory of history around this intellectual end or transcendence, Marx argues that Hegel's philosophy of history is neither active nor political. For Marx there is no transcendence of objectivity, only the reappropriation of labor by humanity. Marx, therefore, unlike Hegel, must pay particular attention to how labor is formed and constrained in history and in production.

Marx was indebted to Hegel for the doctrine that labor is human self-objectification or "man's coming-to-be himself." It is that doctrine which I call the fundamental ontology underlying Marx's research. The concept of self-objectification, however, was reworked by Marx to distinguish the essential character of human activity from the specific social alienations of labor in history. Hegel had obscured this distinction by treating alienation as the necessary fate of all human projects. It was necessary because alienation is what moves Spirit to self-realization, and it was a human fate because freedom involves the transcendence of the limits of human affairs. In this way, Marx argued, Hegel confused historical and ontological conditions. For Marx the alienation of labor is the historical form in which labor's product is appropriated by another through a structure of property and exchange. Though it may appear to those involved as a "fate," this historical form of labor can be reversed by human action itself. Therefore we find in Marx a distinction between labor as essential human activity, as the foundation for all social life, and labor in its historical forms, such as that of slaves, serfs or wage laborers.

The distinction confirms that Marx was not equating the philosophical concept of labor as objectification with economic or utilitarian forms. The form of labor is mediated and modified by the existing social structure, but it is objectification that determines the place of the economic. Only because human objectification confronts humanity as a second nature does it appear, on the contrary, that it is the economy which is determining. "The apparent stupidity of merging all the manifold relationships of people in the *one* relation of usefulness, this apparently metaphysical abstraction arises from the fact that, in modern bourgeois society, all relations are subordinated in practice to the one abstract monetary-commercial relation."[10]

The argument that labor is objectification rather than a simple economic activity in Marx can be further supported by turning to Marx's later position in *Capital*. There we find a most significant passage defining the labor process.

> Labour is, first of all, a process between man and nature, a process by which man, through his own actions, mediates, regulates and controls the metabolism between himself and nature. He confronts the materials of nature as a force of nature. He sets in motion the natural forces which belong to his own body, his arms, legs, head and hands, in order to appropriate the materials of nature in a form adapted to his own needs. Through this movement he acts upon external nature and changes it, and in this way simultaneously changes his own nature.[11]

Marx's presentation cannot be fully understood apart from the ontology of human activity we found partly developed in the *Paris Manuscripts*. Marx begins by repeating Hegel's insight that labor mediates the processes of nature by changing their form. The change of form is precisely the objectification of human purpose in the material world which, in turn, becomes the conditioning structure for the historical forms of life. Marx also distinguishes between the biological or natural instincts and the distinctive human characteristic of action Marx calls purposive activity (*zweckmassige Tätigkeit*).

> We are not dealing here with those first instinctive forms of labour which remain on the animal level. An immense interval of time separates the state of things in which a man brings his labour-power to market for sale as a commodity from the situation when human labour had not yet cast off its first instinctive form. We presuppose labour in a form in which it is an exclusively human characteristic. A spider conducts operations which resemble those of the weaver, and a bee would put many human architects to shame by the construction of its honey comb cells. But what distinguishes the worst architect from the best of bees is that the architect builds the cell in his mind before he constructs it

> in wax. At the end of every labour process, a result
> emerges which had already been conceived by the worker
> at the beginning, hence already existed ideally. Man not
> only effects a change of form in the materials of nature; he
> also realizes his own purpose in those materials. And this is
> a purpose he is conscious of, it determines the mode of activity with the rigidity of a law and he must subordinate his
> will to it.[12]

Therefore the activity of objectification is not just any transformation of the external world but one directed from conscious purpose and end. Since labor is realization of purpose as a mode of activity it is not reducible to a functional or biological reality.

What Marx calls the external and universal condition of human life is the ontological structure of action, the objectification of the subject, and not a biological doctrine of human nature. The ontological structure of action that Marx presupposes in his analysis remains at an abstract level. While it is fundamental to understanding the labor process, it does not tell us what specific historical manifestation of labor we are dealing with. Therefore while it is important to understand this ontology so as to avoid falling into an economic determinism, one must not reason, as Hegel did, that these intellectual categories are the whole reality of human history.

> The labour process, as we have just represented it in its
> simple and abstract elements, is purposive activity amid at
> the production of use-values. It is an appropriation of what
> exists in nature for the requirements of man. It is the universal condition for the metabolic interaction [*Stoffwechsel*]
> between man and nature, the everlasting nature-imposed
> condition of human existence, and it is therefore independent of every form of that existence, or rather it is common
> to all forms of society in which human beings live. . . . The
> taste of porridge does not tell us who grew the oats, and
> the process we have presented does not reveal the conditions under which it takes place, whether it is happening
> under the slave-owner's brutal lash or the anxious eye of
> the capitalist.[13]

The argument that Marx did not embrace economic determinism can now be made more specific. Marx credits political economy with adopting labor as the universal for all societies. But political economy, lacking a theory of human action, considers labor only as economic necessity, that is, only under its present historical form. Since it does not grasp labor as life activity and objectification of the subject, political economy paints a picture of history ruled by the eternal and inexorable laws of the economy. These laws, however, are only the representation of society through the "anxious eyes of the capitalist." "These formulas [the theory of value in political economy], which bear the unmistakable stamp of belonging to a social formation in which the process of production has mastery over man, instead of the opposite, appear to the political economist's bourgeois consciousness to be as much a self-evident and nature-imposed necessity as productive labour itself."[14]

Marx's often reiterated point that political economy is ahistorical really means that political economy lacks a theory of activity. Therefore the laws of political economy are only the appearance of a society in which the activity of objectification and realization are solidified into purely economic exchange. In political economy it is historicity as part of an ontology of social action which is missing.

The main points can now be briefly recapitulated. Marx's concept of labor is a theory of activity or ontology of action which he calls purposive activity, form-giving activity, objectification, or self-realization. The term ontology means that this concept of labor is universal and presupposed by every form of social life. As a concept it precedes the very distinction between the economic and the social. Labor is a process of mediation and therefore is not fixed by nature or what is given; labor as human activity is therefore historical and symbolic. Finally Marx not only rejects the determinism of economic laws proposed by political economy but shows that these laws are the manifestation or appearance of human action reduced by social structure to economic exchange. Determinism reflects then a historical form of activity, not an ontology of action.

From these conclusions we can now turn to the concept of culture. As was already apparent in Hegel, culture is made possible through objectification. It is the realm of objects constituted by humanity as its conditioning world. Culture is inseparable from the distinctive characteristic of purposive action or symbolic mediation. Such an interpretation already makes it impossible to presuppose the separation of culture and the economy sustaining a causal or deterministic account.

It is of course Marx's famous architectural metaphor of superstructure and base that is most often cited on the question of the relation between culture and economy in Marx's thought. This metaphor lends itself to a reductionist interpretation of Marx.

> The general conclusion at which I have arrived and which, once realized, became the guiding principle of my studies can be summarized as follows: In the social production of their existence men inevitably enter into definite relations, which are independent of their will, namely relations of production appropriate to a given stage in the development of their material forces of production. The totality of their relations of production constitutes the economic structure of society, the real foundation, on which arises a legal and political superstructure and to which correspond definite forms of social consciousness. The mode of production of material life conditions the general process of social, political and intellectual life.[15]

The traditional reading perceives this passage as defining two separate spheres of the social structure in a kind of causal relationship. The real foundation designates the economy as causally determining. In my approach the concept of foundation refers to human activity or purposive action. The passage consequently says that the social and historical form of such activity (labor) conditions or sets the limits to the forms of social consciousness. Culture, which is just such an objectification, is therefore conditioned or expressive of the particular organization of human activity that Marx calls a mode of production. Since the objectification of the subject transforms both the object and subject of activity, it is impossible, once one has accepted that ontology, to interpret the superstructural model as a causal one. The reductionist or causal interpretation of this metaphor in Marx mistakenly assumes that, by using the phrase "real foundation," Marx means that the economic base is somehow not cultural and mediated by activity or conversely that the culture or superstructure is therefore not real.

It would be reasonable to assume that the reading of Marx we have constructed should find an application where Marx speaks about culture and superstructure. In fact in a very significant passage we find culture treated not only as purposive action or form-giving activity—therefore not separate from labor as objectification—but as relatively autonomous from economic development. "In the case of the arts, it is well known that certain periods of their flowering are all out of proportion to the general development of society, hence also to the material foundation, the skeletal structure, as it were, of its organization."[16]

Such a statement would be hard to fit into the economistic model of interpretation since culture is not treated as the mirror of economic progress. But underlying this passage is Marx's basic definition of mode of production as a mode of life activity and not an economic function. "Thus mode of production must not be considered simply as being the reproduction of the physical existence of the individual. Rather it is a definite form of activity of these individuals, a definite form of expressing their life, a definite mode of life on their part. As individuals express their life, so they are."[17]

Culture constitutes a mode of expression of life conditioned by the form of production or form of life activity. Marx was aware that these were statements at the ontological level and therefore did not try to relate this social ontology immediately to the explanation of the historical relationship between culture and production. In fact Marx seems to warn against such an a priori approach and the historical specificity it leaves out.

> But the difficulty lies not in understanding that the Greek arts and epic are bound up with certain forms of social development. The difficulty is that they still afford us artistic pleasure and that in a certain respect they count as a norm and as an unattainable model. A man cannot become a child again, or he becomes childish. But does he not find joy in the child's naïveté, and must he himself not strive to reproduce its truth at a higher stage? Does not the true character of each epoch come alive in the nature of its children? Why should not the historical childhoods of humanity, its most beautiful unfolding, as a stage never to return, exercise an eternal charm? There are unruly children and precocious children. Many of the old peoples belong in this category. The Greeks were normal children. The charm of their art for us is not in contradiction to the undeveloped stage of society in which it grew. It is its result, rather, and is inextricably bound up, rather, with the fact that the unripe social conditions under which it arose, and could alone arise can never return.[18]

Marx wanted to disassociate his views from any nostalgia for a "golden age" or glorification of the Greek *polis*, which was common in German philosophy at the time. However, he does intend to show that in the formation of culture and economy simple relations of correspondence do not hold. Precisely the undeveloped character of material production can produce a flowering of cultural production. Correspondingly a highly developed economic structure, like commodity production, can cripple cultural expression and the realization of a rich or complex mode of life. The problem is that while both labor and culture are forms of objectification in Marx's theory there is no single relationship between them. Marx's metaphor of culture as the superstructure over the economic base was an attempt to handle this indeterminate relationship.

Instead of explaining events through a causal analysis, Marx developed a theory of action. Expressed in the language of objectification and mediation, Marx explained the relationship between labor and society through the symbolic or meaningful character of action. From the vantage point of such an interpretation objectification in economic activity is not radically different from objectification in the realm of culture. In this way we retain Marx's position that society is best approached as a totality and that it represents more than an aggregate of individual actions. In this context Marx's superstructure/base distinction loses the status it has in orthodox Marxist interpretation. Marx does no more than state the problem of the complex relationship between economic and cultural activity. Marx saw that by using the theory of labor he could dispense with the obsolete explanations invoking human nature or social contract. However, he did not develop the theory of labor, aside from suggestions, beyond his critique of political economy. In the modern era of social theory and the total eclipse of political economy as a discipline, Marx's critique has lost its object. To continue to repeat Marx's analysis of the labor process in purely economic terms is to play into the hands of a narrow economistic and utilitarian view of society. What Marx did to the conception of the economy in the nineteenth century must now be done with regard to culture in the twentieth century.

Marx did not fully clarify the model of explanation he practiced. His argument was that society cannot be understood as a wholly external object in the grasp of inexorable laws. The very theory we articulate is implicated in the object of study, since social consciousness is just as much a product of social forces as of material needs. Therefore theory, or what Marx calls the self-consciousness of a society or culture, is not outside but inside the field of objectifications and activities that make up the totality of social relations.

The unification of theory and practice is the slogan that is supposed to explain the role of theory in classical Marxism. But as with most famous phrases in philosophy, Marx's assertion is notoriously vague. Certainly Marx did not mean that theory would be judged in terms of its practical consequences, nor did he mean that a successful theory is one that produces political results. There is no hint of pragmatism in Marx when it comes to the judgment of theory, and he seems to have gone out of his way to show how his theoretical research brought him into profound disagreement with his avowed political supporters. Certainly the position appears to mean, as we have shown, that theory is somehow part of the social forms of objectification in which a society shapes and is shaped by human activity.

It would seem that, like superstructure and base, the appeal to the unification of theory and practice is a metaphor for a model of explanation that Marx did not clarify. But we can say more about this relationship by noting that there is a profound political meaning to Marx's view of theoretical activity. Marx's primary aim was to understand how exploitation functioned in modern society and correlatively how society conceals or masks its social relations. Every society therefore is the establishment of a specific mode of action or labor and the imposition of that mode of action by making it appear natural or immutable. Marx found this strategy at work in the ahistorical attitude of classical political economy and its appeal to "iron laws" of the economy.

Marx wanted to account for the effect of society on consciousness through the term ideology. With the use of this term Marx tried to study and explain how thought stands in relation to a society when it is, no matter what its intention, reinforcing that social order. Ideology implies first of all that thinking involves a set of ideas which are specifically distorted or obscured in their vision of the world. The inaccuracy of an ideologists' picture of the world is not arbitrary since its specific distortion serves to justify and legitimize the society. Marx's favorite examples involve the philosophical and religious traditions of dualism and divided reality. Divisions such as the secular and the heavenly in religion or appearance and reality in philosophy reveal a common theme of relegating the problematic aspects of life to the realm of illusion and placing the reality of our human world in an inaccessible and supra-human realm. Though he was well aware that this approach was a vast oversimplification for all but minor figures in the history of thought, Marx assumed that some such explanation would ultimately make clear the social function of philosophy and religion.

The problem with the concept of ideology is not that it oversimplifies the role of theory. More seriously the model of ideas representing or picturing an external world, either accurately or in a "camera obscura" as Marx says, does not do justice to Marx's insight that theory is an objectifying activity. In using the term "ideology" Marx reinforced the view of theory as a passive effect of certain causal forces. It was natural that Marxism should in the twentieth century canonize this under a wider deterministic doctrine.

2. The Economic and the Symbolic in Culture

THE interpretation outlined in chapter 1 is intended as a philosophical position attributed to Marx on the question of the nature of society. It by no means serves as the only representation of Marx's intentions or intellectual contribution. Marx's continuing relevance is not due, I think, to the prophetic character of his writings. Rather in Marx we find the initiation of our present understanding of what a society is and how it functions; he stands between the present and the heterogeneous doctrines of natural law, contract theory, and divine rule of the past. I do not imply that all social theory is thus contained in the writings of Marx, any more than all natural science is contained in the first attempts by Galileo to articulate a new physics. Indeed, when a new strategy for inquiry has begun or a new set of concepts is formulated, the answers are not suddenly obvious and apparent. Marx did, however, initiate a new direction for research and inquiry, although the process by which he extricated himself from his heritage and forged the concepts for the study of society was neither simple nor of a piece. What we see in Marx's writings is partly the record of laborious criticism and reformulation.

In trying to make Marx's position sharper my intention is not purely exegetical: I want to look at how Marx is used and criticized by certain contemporary theorists who are concerned, as Marx was, with the question of the foundation of society and history. Consequently, though I return to Marx in this chapter, the problems and questions posed could neither have occurred to Marx nor have been possible at that time. In fact the central problem I have chosen, the nature of culture and what Marx called the superstructure, pushes at the limits of his thought; there is very little available in Marx's writings on this topic, and what he does say is vague and open to wide interpretation. At the same time it is precisely the so-called Marxist account of superstructure and culture that is most problematic and often disputed. Thus the inadequacies of Marx's account of culture and an attempt to reformulate his ideas are the focus of the discussion to follow.

Marx, we must remember, envisioned a grand project. He intended to produce a complete study of modern society, including the formation and role of the State, Law, Philosophy, and Religion. The economic studies, which were all that Marx ever completed, were to have been only the first volume of this projected research. As we know, even that portion was only partly completed. In other words, Marx left nothing of what would have been most interesting to modern social theory. Yet such a judgment is somewhat premature, as I will try to show, since the economic writings do contain hints at least of the intended larger analysis. But it is true that on the broader issues of social philosophy Marx relegated his thoughts more and more toward general comments, metaphors, and marginal notes.

In his notes to himself, Marx expressed some doubts about his previous account of cultural development and its relation to economic development; he was aware that the judgment of all societies from the vantage point of capitalist production was inherently distorting, as is evident in his constant criticism of British political economy. Also Marx became extremely interested at the end of his life in the work of the American anthropologist Lewis Henry Morgan. Although Marx searched Morgan's work initially for confirmation of the historical materialist method, new questions were inevitably raised. The culture of so-called primitive societies appeared highly complex and intricate, and economic activity, when isolated, did not appear to fall easily into Marx's general category of primitive communism. Moreover, Marx had hoped to explain the "laws" for the transition from one mode of production to another. Though Marx could not have fully appreciated it at the time, the emergence of anthropology and other associated social sciences would make that search for a single body of laws less likely. No matter how fallible we consider such new fields as social psychology, archeology, comparative anthropology, and even psychoanalysis, by virtue of their investigations we are in a much stronger position to talk about the formation, complexity, and function of culture. In view of this increasing complexity, what relevance does the theory of labor have for modern social theory? Does Marx's metaphor of "superstructure" satisfactorily explain the function of culture as we know it today?

I began with a presentation separating Marx from economic determinism narrowly understood. In this chapter I want to go further and suggest that within what Marx wrote about economic structure, there is the beginning of a theory of cultural forms or modes of expression. Since we can go no further with Marx alone, I believe, the discussion will turn to how Marx has been appropriated and transformed by a group of contemporary social philosophers. The writings of Jean Joseph Goux and Jean Baudrillard and the joint theory of Gilles Deleuze and Felix Guattari represent three important interpretations that are part of a single tradition of contemporary French social philosophy. They will be the focus of the next three chapters. I have chosen them because I believe their accounts are interconnected and not well known in English philosophy. Yet their syntheses of Marx and social theory are dramatic and important. Other theorists could certainly have been chosen, for example, Hannah Arendt and Jurgen Habermas or the impact of Marxism in anthropology through such current theorists as Marshall Sahlins or Marvin Harris. But I have purposely shifted the emphasis to the more theoretical and philosophical French tradition. I do not intend by that to downplay the role of investigation and research over against theoretical speculation. I want to use the space of this short study to return to the *idea* of a society or culture. What makes social and cultural life possible? This question does not provide a solution to methodological and procedural problems of research, but it does supply the framework around which social research can continue.

I shall discuss a passage from Marx's *Capital* that extends the approach I have outlined in the first chapter and explains what I mean by Marx's theory of cultural forms or the objectivity of social forms. I then present a reading of Claude Levi-Strauss' concept of "symbolic effectiveness." By shifting to Levi-Strauss I want first to emphasize some current problems in philosophy of the social sciences concerning the nature of explanation for social life. While Marx could not have foreseen what Levi-Strauss means by culture as a symbolic system, the philosophical or theoretical issues are connected. Also Levi-Strauss brings out very clearly, in the example I have chosen, the role of symbolic structure in social control and cohesion. I believe Marx had a very similar insight into the formation of political and cultural hegemony. Third, all of the interpreters I have chosen to discuss are

The Economic and the Symbolic in Culture

profoundly influenced and indebted to Levi-Strauss' theories and research on primitive societies. Therefore the thought of Levi-Strauss runs like a thread through the remaining chapters. My exposition will provide a unifying reference point along with the material on Marx.

Symbolic Effectiveness

Levi-Strauss develops the concept of *l'efficacité symbolique* in an article on shamanism which describes the narrative song (as well as ritual actions) employed by a shaman in dealing with a difficult childbirth. Shamanistic practices involve "cures" through "sham battles" or recitations of incantations and prescribed actions. The status of this "therapy" is therefore difficult to grasp, since the actions are too crude to result in a cure and the abstract ritual does not seem to have any bearing on illness. The question Levi-Strauss poses is whether we can grasp "how specific psychological representations are invoked to combat equally specific disturbances." According to his analysis, the shamanistic recitation or song reconnects the patient's physiological reactions to a mythic struggle over the woman's soul. Hence, it is directed primarily at a *prise de conscience* on the part of the patient which will indirectly produce the hoped-for physiological response. "Everything occurs as though the shaman were trying to induce the woman—whose contact with reality is no doubt impaired and whose sensitivity is exacerbated—to relive the initial situation through pain, in a very precise and intense way, and to become psychologically aware of its smallest details."[1]

As Levi-Strauss indicates, in this way the myth "names" the process so as to present it in a *form* accessible to the woman's consciousness. The myth, which is primarily a social dimension and practice, allows manipulation *but only* through the symbolic realm, through meaning equivalents which nonetheless have an efficacy and force in reality:[2] an efficacy and force very different from medical treatment and not reducible to physical manipulation. "The technique of the narrative thus aims at recreating a real experience in which the myth shifts the protagonists . . . to make the center of inexpressible and painful sensations 'clear' to her and accessible to her consciousness . . . enables them to relate in detail a complicated itinerary that is a true mythical anatomy corresponding less to the real structure of the genital organs than to a kind of emotional geography."[3]

But if pains are thus given a meaning and coherence, why does that entail a physiological reaction? In other words, merely explaining to someone that his disease is the result of viruses does not in itself produce health. Why should the coherence of mythic categories produce, simply because they are strongly believed by both the shaman and the patient, a physiological change? The point is that these are two separate forms of explanation, one which is concerned with explaining why a birth is difficult (and is external to the birth act itself) and a second which is solely concerned with how the woman understands and deals with these experiences (and is therefore inseparable from the actual birth event). The "cure" Levi-Strauss is investigating is a symbolic manipulation,[4] that is, a physiological change as the by-product of approaching the patient through physiological events presented in their meaningful and significant equivalents, in their already (socially) mediated symbolic form.

> [T]he relation between microbes and sickness is external to the patient's mind, it is a cause and effect relation; whereas the relation between monsters and sickness is interior to the conscious or unconscious mind itself; it is a relation of symbol to thing symbolized, or . . . of signifier to signified. The shaman furnishes a *language* to the sick person, in which otherwise inexpressible states can be immediately expressed. And it is this passage to verbal expression (which permits, simultaneously, living through in an intelligible and ordered form an actual experience which would otherwise be chaotic and ineffable) which induces the release of the physiological process, that is, the reorganization, in a favorable direction, of the sequence of events to which the patient is subjected.[5]

The experience is provoked through language; it is concerned with the patient's access to meaning (physiological responses are sought through a level of symbolic manipulation), and the process involves some form of transference. As usual, Levi-Strauss draws a connection with psychoanalysis. "When a transference is established, the patient puts words into the mouth of the psychoanalyst by attributing to him alleged feelings and intentions; in the incantations, on the contrary, the shaman speaks for his patient. He questions her and puts into her mouth answers that correspond to the interpretations of her condition which she must come to see through [*se penetrer*]."[6]

Of course, the point of this article is a reiteration of the major Levi-

Straussian themes: the unconscious is a symbolic function (invariant with regard to diverse social systems); it is structured like a discourse; and its form dominates all content. The shaman-psychoanalyst analogy seems particularly effective in demonstrating what it means to say: that the symbolic realm of society is productive, that it possesses an efficacy of reproduction of the social relations that is more binding than force or coercion. Levi-Strauss argues that even where certain physiological events are invariant, there is always a residue of meaning that is generated in a cultural system through what appear to be biological and fixed processes. Whether we are dealing with illness, eating, or procreation, the biological aspect of the act is overcoded with significances. These meanings, which convert events into signs, are the consequence of existing both as a biological being and an *animal symbolicum*.

To argue that the symbolic is the structure that binds together the life processes of the society does not simply mean that such fixed, physiological events are given different names by different cultures. The claim that the symbolic realm of meaning and equivalence is productive, in much the way we speak of material production, is specifically that it *forms* needs and desires with a determinateness comparable to the physiological substratum necessary for any society. Therefore "symbolic effectiveness" concerns the connectedness or cohesion of the disparate levels of social reality. It is clear that Levi-Strauss does not intend, in his own theoretical work, to develop the social specificity of the concept or its role in reproduction of social relations. However, this definition certainly speaks to those issues: "Symbolic effectiveness would consist precisely in this 'inductive property' by which formally homologous structures, built out of different levels of life—organic processes, unconscious mind, rational thought are related to one another."[7]

The insight here is not only that the materiality and productiveness of symbolization and meaning equivalence are emphasized but that the symbolic dimension is identified as the *place* in which physiology is mediated (socially). As a place of manipulation the subject's desires and needs (the areas of sexuality, maturation, consumption, etc.), in spite of their biological continuity, enter into the reproduction of diverse social formations in diverse modes of expression. Levi-Strauss shows that the dimensions of sexuality, need, and biological function are, for any society, not a matter of physiology but first a matter of symbolic manipulation.

Levi-Strauss approached society through its exchange processes because exchange is the expression of a society as a symbolic system. "All culture can be considered as a whole of symbolic systems at the first level of which is language, matrimonial rules, economic relations, art, science, religion. All these systems seek to express certain aspects of the physical and social reality and the relation between these two types of reality."[8] The aim of a social theory, for Levi-Strauss, is to reduce the seemingly diverse appearances of social life to universal structures for all culture. These universal structures, even though unconscious, actually determine the details of cultural forms and are investigated as a collective manifestation of meaning. "It is in the nature of society that it expresses itself symbolically in its customs and in its institutions; on the other hand normal individual conduct is never symbolic by itself; individual conduct is only one element out of which a symbolic system, which can only be collective, is constituted."[9]

We find, for example, in Levi-Strauss' first major work, *The Elementary Structures of Kinship*, the investigation of the problem of the transition from nature to culture. Levi-Strauss, in his search for universals underlying all societies, views such universals as manifested, at least in primitive societies, in the rules for marriage and exchange of women. "What are the mental structures to which we have referred and the universality of which we believe can be established? It seems there are three: the exchange of the rule as a rule; the notion of reciprocity regarded as the most immediate form of integrating the opposition between self and other; and finally, the synthetic nature of the gift."[10]

Therefore, we could say that for Levi-Strauss, the infrastructure of society is not the mode of production or labor process but the universality, among humans, of symbolic systems. Such systems are like language and ultimately are explained through mental structure. Consequently Levi-Strauss holds the naturalistic assumption that innate mental structure explains social activities. When Levi-Strauss acknowledges his debt to Marx, it is not to the theory of labor but to Marx's anti-empiricism. Marx realized, Levi-Strauss argues, that social relations were not observable, and therefore he directed our attention to the lawful and universal regularities underlying cultural diversity. Therefore if Levi-Strauss calls his own work a contribution to the study of superstructure, as he does in *The Savage Mind*, it is only after making a central qualification of Marx's theory. "Marxists, if not Marx himself, have too commonly reasoned as though practice followed directly

The Economic and the Symbolic in Culture 23

from *praxis*. Without questioning the undoubted primacy of infrastructure, I believe there is always a mediator between *praxis* and practice, namely the conceptual scheme by the operation of which form and matter, neither with any independent existence, are realized as structures. . . . But in order for *praxis* to be even thought, it is necessary first (in a logical and not historical sense) for thought to exist; that is to say, its initial conditions must be given in the form of the objective structure of the psyche and brain without which there would be neither *praxis* nor thought."[11]

Levi-Strauss' argument is that if Marx appeals to labor as the foundation of society he fails to recall that labor is already prefigured by physiological and mental structures independently of any social system. As we have already seen, however, Marx does not appeal to naturalistic explanations of society or labor. Certainly Marx understood that nature precedes and constrains the development of society.

As early as *German Ideology*, Marx draws attention to the role of geography and the natural, biological foundations of social life. But even at this point Marx is also arguing against such naturalists as Ludwig Feuerbach and the utilitarians. Marx speaks in *German Ideology*, for example, about the "first historical act" being the creation of new needs. He explicitly argues against the doctrine of any invariant human nature and attacks Feuerbach's concept of man's species-being (*Gattungswesen*) as anti-historical. Such positions, which become even more clear in Marx's later writings, suggest that Marx did not conceive of a direct impact of nature on society. In effect the impact of nature is always mediated or itself conditioned by purposive human action (*Zweckmassige Tätigkeit*).

In Levi-Strauss we find a reductionist position. Explanations of culture and society will eventually be reduced to, or be nothing more than, explanations at the biological and physiological level. Even though Marx also spoke of discovering "laws" of society and history, he did not adopt the reductionist approach. First, what Marx meant by law we would now call a trend or tendency, especially in economics. In other words, it is the framework in which action takes place; therefore a law, in Marx's sense, constrains but does not predetermine human action. Second, Marx's aim was not the discovery of what is invariant in all culture. His aim was to define how societies organized to control and legitimize the exercise of exploitive power. Therefore, unlike Levi-Strauss' studies of superstructure, the center of Marx's analyses is the role of mystification, false consciousness, and what he calls ideology. In Levi-Strauss we find no social importance given to the manner in which a society distorts or misreads its own activities. For Levi-Strauss that is due simply to the fact that universal structures are unconscious "rules," frequently inaccessible to the person who uses them. Even in passages where Marx emphasizes the conditioning of the human subject, as in this one, it is clear that the symbolic dimension refers to activity rather than innate mental structure.

> The more deeply we go back into history, the more does the individual, and hence also the producing individual, appear as dependent, as belonging to a greater whole; in a still quite natural way in the family and in the family expanded into the clan. . . . Only in the eighteenth century . . . do the various forms of social connectedness confront the individual as a mere means toward his private purpose, as external necessity. But the epoch which produces this standpoint, that of the isolated individual, is also precisely that of the hitherto most developed social . . . relations. The human being is . . . an animal which can individualize itself in the midst of society. Production by an isolated individual outside of society . . . is as much an absurdity as is the development of language without individuals living together and talking to one another.[12]

In placing the emphasis on the role of mystification or false consciousness in Marx's account of forms of consciousness, I have intentionally pointed to the absence of this concept in Levi-Strauss' theory of symbolism. The ultimate concern of Levi-Strauss' concept of symbolic effectiveness is not social structure (though it is applicable) but the structure of mind as that is manifested in cultural universals. Levi-Strauss has consistently argued for the reduction of the human sciences into the natural sciences. He presents his object of inquiry not in terms of the separation between culture and nature, as Marx does with labor as the *differentia specifica* of human existence, but as the universal mental forms that constitute all possible cultures.

> An ideal analysis . . . may allow the natural to be isolated from the cultural element . . . then . . . everything universal in man relates to the natural order, and is characterized by spontaneity, and . . . everything subject to norm is cultural and is both relative and particular. We are then confronted with a fact, or rather, a group of facts which, in

the light of the previous definition, are not far removed from a scandal; we refer to that complex group of beliefs, customs, conditions and institutions described succinctly as the prohibition of incest, which presents, without the slightest ambiguity, and inseparably combined, the two characteristics in which we recognize the conflicting features of two mutually exclusive orders. It constitutes a rule, but a rule which alone among social rules, possesses at the same time a universal character. . . . Here therefore is a phenomenon which has the distinctive characteristics of both nature and of its theoretical contradiction, culture. The prohibition of incest has the universality of bent and instinct and the coercive character of law and institution.[13]

I turned to an example from Levi-Strauss to explain why Marx's concept of labor should be taken as symbolic. Labor is what Levi-Strauss calls a system of exchange and not a utilitarian struggle with nature. However, the direction in which Levi-Strauss proceeds with his analysis is completely different from Marx. Levi-Strauss takes a step backward in pursuing a reductionist approach to social explanation. But more significant it is the absence in Levi-Strauss' work of any treatment of what Marx called ideology that makes Levi-Strauss' insights into symbolic exchange sterile for a social theory. Therefore we now turn to how Marx carried out an analysis of social exchange processes and their impact on social consciousness.

Commodity-Form

The analysis of the commodity, which is the foundation of Marx's critique of political economy, is also the presentation of a homologous *form* through which a social formation relates disparate practices on the basis of a specific mode of production. But the commodity is not only the "inductive property" that Levi-Strauss describes linking through its "efficacy," social life and economic utility; it is also a "fantastic form" concealing what is not equivalent—that for which there is no exchange. The dynamic of concealment in this "social hieroglyphics," which secured social reproduction at the level of consciousness, is precisely the point of *critique* in Marx. It is precisely this critical, social aspect of form that is missing in the example from Levi-Strauss. I will now show how equivalence and form operate in Marx's analysis.

Marx approaches exchange value as the process by which diverse products are given a uniform social status as commodities distinct from their varied *forms* of existence as use values. Hence exchange value is a form of equivalence—a comparative analysis of objects through a common denominator. Value allows objects to function and circulate in a specific *social form*. "Value, therefore, does not have its description branded on its forehead; it rather transforms every product of labour into a social hieroglyphic. Later on, men try to decipher the hieroglyphic, to get behind the secret of their own social product: for the characteristic which objects of utility have of being values is as much men's social product as is their language."[14]

The secret of the social product is the value form—the abstract equivalence of exchange. But that form is the product of a specific practice. This practice is labor-power as homogeneous, abstract, and equivalent. Thus in labor as in all commodities the qualitative distinctness of utility is eliminated through "equal exchange magnitudes." This form of equivalence is realized in the act of exchange and in that way expresses an identity (form as abstraction) between labor and the commodity-form.

> Quite irrespective, therefore, of their natural form of existence, and without regard to the specific character of the needs they satisfy as use-values, commodities in definite quantities are congruent, they take one another's place in the exchange process, are regarded as equivalents, and despite their motley appearance have a common denominator. . . . As exchange-values in which the qualitative difference between their use-value is eliminated, they represent equal amounts of the same kind of labour. . . . they represent the same homogeneous labour, i.e. labour in which the individual characteristics of the worker are obliterated. Labour which creates exchange-value is thus abstract *general* labour.[15]

Of course this concept of abstraction is used by Marx in the Hegelian sense and is therefore not merely an operation in thought. It is, as Marx says, "an abstraction which is made every day in the social process of production." This process of abstraction has two moments. The product is abstracted from the natural form of utility while labour, the activity, is abstracted from all organic and social limitations which stand against the universalizing tendency of the value-form. The important point, the distinctive feature of Marx's theory of subjectivity and production, is the distortive and mystifying function of the equivalence-form. "Human labour-power in its fluid state, or human labour, creates value, but is not itself value. It becomes value in its coagulated state, in objective form. The value of linen as a congealed mass of human labour can be expressed only as an 'objectivity' [*Gegenstandlichkeit*], a thing which is materially different from the linen itself and yet common to the linen and other commodities. . . . Here is therefore a thing in which value is manifested, or which represents value in its tangible, natural form."[16]

Here we see the equivalence-form as the motor force for allowing activities and objects to have the same form and thus the same social meaning. But simultaneously it misrepresents this reproduction so that labor does *appear* as a value, so that human activity does exist only in the form of some object. Therefore, while human subjectivity is mediated through a symbolic function (and consequently the error of all economistic readings of Marx's categories), that creation of meaning has an ambivalent function of concealment which introduces control and manipulation of those activities. Whereas this appears neutral, benevolent, and even asocial in Levi-Strauss, in Marx it is directly tied to a critical assault on the form and limits of human activities and of human subjectivity in relation to social control.

The value expression does not appear as a social relation since the commodity appears to express value in itself, endowed with the property of exchangeability from Nature. Conversely the limiting and formation of human activities appear not as acts of social control and domination but as a direct result of its immutable, inherent nature. As mediation the equivalence-form, like symbolic manipulation, turns a physiological act into a symbolic, meaningful practice. In this case it turns concrete labor into the manifestation of abstract human labor and therefore the labor of private individuals into "labor directly social in its form." Finally this whole mediation does not appear to consciousness, which, in an inversion, returns it to the physiological. In Marx's interpretation the value-form and the equivalence-form function as a mediation for separate social spheres and a reproduction of social subjectivity. The commodity is simultaneously an exchange value and a *hieroglyphics* of social relations—it is literally a text.

Marx gives the fullest discussion of the equivalence-form in his treatment of the genesis of money. The argument is that the universal equivalent emerges through a series of social acts by which products are converted into commodities and commodities into money. Marx characterizes this process not as a historical series but as an idealization of the abstraction process latent in the exchange of equivalents. There is a coincidence between the logical and historical moments of this process as embodied in the commodity.

> Money necessarily crystallizes out of the process of exchange, in which different products of labour are in fact equated with each other, and thus converted into commodities. The historical broadening and deepening of the phenomenon of exchange develops the opposition between use-value which is latent in the nature of the commodity. The need to give an external expression to this opposition for the purposes of commercial intercourse produces the drive towards an independent form of value, which finds neither rest nor peace until an independent form has been achieved by the differentiation of commodities into commodities and money. At the same rate, then, as the transformation of the products of labour into commodities is accomplished, one particular commodity is transformed into money.[17]

In this movement toward equivalent exchange and the money-form Marx distinguishes three stages. The first is elementary barter, where exchange is a matter of chance and where a rough distinction between objects for consumption and exchange acquires the *stamp of custom*—rather than the designation of value. Clearly it is precisely the accidental character of exchange and its *control* or limitation through custom (that is, the dominance of a noneconomic structure) which is progressively overcome in the next stages. The extent of the coincidence between the logical and historical moments can be suggested by using Weber's term of "rationalization" to describe what happens to the exchange process as it is separated from customary control and forms a purely quantitative concept of equivalence.

The second stage involves an increase in the number and variety of objects exchanged. As both labor and production in general increase in complexity, there is a need for commodities to be exchanged for and equated with a single article. However, this state retains a trace of arbitrariness by designating the "special article" with a value which is not entirely economic and quantitative. These objects of prestige, totemic status, or political power are what Marx calls "the general social

The Economic and the Symbolic in Culture   29

equivalent," and within the limits of a pre-market society (in Marx's sense of the term) they function to rationalize the exchange process.

In the third state exchange becomes autonomous from capricious customary limitation but therefore completely quantitative and abstract. That process is expressed by saying that value must take on the specifics of the value-form. What is significant about this typology, which is certainly not original with Marx, is his concluding argument that the process by which exchange passes into the equivalence-form is itself an expression of the more fundamental change in which labor passes from its concrete to its abstract social form. Thus the necessity or efficacy which works itself out in this typology of exchange is the act of production or labor in a new *form*. It is the combination of this concept of *form* and the labor process that is the distinctive aspect of Marx's theory of society. Therefore we see that one aspect of the efficacy of the equivalence-form is its destruction of all natural and customary restraints on production and labor. That is, it frees labor from religious, familial, or social-customary limitations. Therefore when Marx calls the creation of abstract labor contradictory, he means that on the one hand it reifies labor under the dominance of the value-form and reduces it to an economic quantification of exchange, but at the same time this abstraction liberates human productivity, energy, and labor power from the narrow dominance of kinship and religion. It is precisely this liberating aspect of the transition from concrete, particular acts of labor to labor-power in general that is given a theoretical expression in societies where human equality becomes a "fixed popular opinion." The privatization of the laborer (which accompanies the homogeneity of labor-power) is the force that expels the vestiges of extra-economic domination over production, characteristic of pre-capitalist societies, and allows the equivalence-form characteristic of capitalist reproduction to enter directly into social relations.

> In the same proportion as exchange bursts its local bonds and the value of commodities accordingly expands more and more into the material embodiment of human labour as such, in that proportion does the money-form become transferred to commodities which are by nature fitted to perform the social function of universal equivalent. . . . we have seen that the money-form is merely the reflection thrown by a single commodity of the relations between all commodities. . . . The process of exchange gives to the

commodity, which it has converted into money, not its value but its specific value-form.[18]

When a specific commodity is crystallized as money its "bodily-form" takes on a power and value which is both mysterious and yet naturalized. In its occult power to manipulate, to determine significance and mediate life—the "*galvano-chemical* power of society," as Marx calls it—money is the culmination of the efficacy of the commodity-form. It is an efficacy whose logic is to simultaneously conceal and thereby reproduce its reality. It is this double movement of effectiveness that is Marx's critical theory of social forms. As he says, "The intermediate steps of the process *vanish in the result* and leave *no trace behind*. Commodities find their own value already completely represented. . . . Hence the magic of money." The "magic" here is not the shamanistic manipulation of consciousness through symbolism but the amnesia, the "lack of trace" through which a form takes on its "fantastic imaginary" power.[19]

In a famous remark Marx specified the "difference" that arises in the historical satisfaction of needs. The remark intends to show how production creates the very nature and character of the needs to be satisfied. Marx had in mind his own analysis of how a new subjectivity is mediated through commodity production (the category used in the *Grundrisse* is personal independence), thereby revealing historically, for the first time, the self-production of the subject through laboring activity. "Hunger is hunger, but the hunger gratified by cooked meat eaten with a knife and fork is a *different hunger* from that which bolts down raw meat with the aid of hand, nail and tooth. . . . Production not only supplies the material for the need, but it also supplies the need for the material." Marx's conclusion from this could serve as the focus for the rest of this study: "Production produces not only the object but also the manner of consumption, not only objectively but also subjectively."[20]

The Mode of Symbolization

Marx's account of the formation of society stresses that, in social exchange, it is the form that determines the status of objects and persons. A commodity is not a simple object but is a complex and mediated social relation. The analysis of the commodity must precede therefore an investigation of its meaning. The commodity is a social hieroglyphics rather than a social mechanism. In Marx's analysis, objects belong neither exclusively to the economy nor to the culture since the separation of economy and culture is an effect rather than a cause of the commodity-form.

In *Economie et Symbolique*, a work influenced by Levi-Strauss and Marx, Jean-Joseph Goux tries to explain in broad terms the role of symbolism in the construction of a social theory. Goux is dissatisfied with the traditional Marxist account of superstructure and base. That schema implies that the symbolic realm comprises the superstructure while the economic base is its real referent or causal agent. For Goux there are two problems with this account. First, it depends on a simple mechanical account of the formation of culture. However, given a single set of economic conditions, there are any number of historical modes of expression and symbolism that could arise. Meaning cannot be reduced to some determined response because the realm of the symbolic is just as much an active transformation and modification of its world as it is a passive response. Second, while Marx analyzed the economic realm in a systematic and theoretical manner, the superstructure remains a bare metaphor. At the level of abstraction the superstructure is treated as a mere list of activities—philosophy, law, religion, morality—without that raised to a comprehension of the underlying structural order of this realm of social life.

For Goux the term *symbolic* refers not to a specific domain of society but to the underlying logic that organizes and unifies each sphere of society. Marx had demonstrated that the economy is a system of meaning, a symbolic order, as we found in his presentation of the commodity-form and the theory of value. Now, argues Goux, we must do the same for the area of the cultural superstructure and the theory of ideology. Goux proceeds by dividing society into three symbolic dimensions—the economy, systems of signs (writing, inscription, and recording), and sexuality, meaning those aspects of maturation and procreation that have symbolic, not purely biological, meaning. The spheres of sexuality and writing comprise what Marx vaguely called the superstructure. For example, writing would include all forms of inscription such as are found in literature, the mass media, philosophy, or law. Instead of studying each of these particular instances, we would study the *form* or the *underlying* order that rules the use of signs and words in any given historical period. Marx, in studying the economy, did not catalogue each particular economic act or exchange but looked for a theory that would explain the underlying dynamic. So Goux concludes that we must approach the superstructure with the same spirit of abstraction.

The domain of sexuality, for example, would encompass not merely the study of reproduction, which Engels has already recognized as a necessary supplement to the study of production in any society, but would also explain such ideological structures as religion, morality, and division of labor. In this way the symbolic dimension of sexuality can be shown to interact with the structure of law or religion in both role and function. It is certainly apparent that Goux has Freud in mind when he expands this interpretation of the domain of sexuality. Goux's approach opens up the enormous topic of the relation between Marx and Freud. I cannot hope to discuss that here, but I do want to show why Freud is used by Goux to fill in the gaps in Marx's account of ideology and political control.

The two spheres of sexuality and writing are shown by Goux to be interconnected, and the link between these is through the function of symbolism and *form*. Marx had already demonstrated that the economy manifests itself as an economic form (the commodity). Therefore, by extending such an analysis to the domain of the superstructure, Goux thinks that we can account for the relationships between culture and the economy without a crude theory of causation or reduction.

A mode of production is the combination and unity of the economy, the sphere of writing or inscription, and the social production of human sexuality. By saying that each of these spheres is a mode of symbolization, Goux wants to stress that each, including the economy, shares a unifying form. Goux is of course attacking the view of Marx as an economic determinist, a position he calls "economism." Economism attempts to reduce the explanation of all social phenomena to the economic because it believes that all culture is a mere reflection of economic forces and that the economy is a physical or natural process excluding the dimension of meaning or symbolic form. In addition to rejecting the economistic picture of society Goux's model is meant to eliminate the use of biological or naturalistic modes of explanation in the superstructure. If we view sexuality as a symbolic or primarily social activity, then we reject explanations at the biological or physiological level. Perhaps we should say that biological or physiological aspects of sexuality exist for the social theorist in their symbolic mediation as they enter into the exchange system or equivalence forms of the society in much the same way that the economic "facts" of money, price, and utility only exist for Marx in their manifestation as commodities and the meaning of that form for social relationships and exchange.

In a famous sociological study, *The Protestant Ethic and the Spirit of Capitalism*, Max Weber demonstrated a connection between the rise and consolidation of the capitalist economy in the West and certain modifications in religious practices. Specifically he showed that a disciplined labor force found its spiritual analogy in asceticism, the renunciation of pleasure, and the emphasis on duty in various Protestant sects. Weber was anxious to show that, unlike Marxism, sociology should not assume that it was the economy that "caused" these changes in religion. Neither the religious (cultural) nor the economic change came first, and therefore a causal analysis, looking for priority in time and the singular production of effects, was inappropriate to social inquiry.

The historical example that Weber investigated, since it uses implicitly a Freudian account of religion, provides strong evidence for the kind of connections Goux has proposed. Goux, however, would like to do more than provide a model to be studied inductively through historical examples. He hopes to provide a general theory of society rather than the account of specific cases, and he hopes to offer more than Weber's dissatisfaction with the causal account. Weber has shown that there is a relationship between these phenomena but remains vague, as Marx was, on just how that relationship takes place. If, as Goux agrees, Marx was not arguing for the economistic position that Weber attributes to Marxism, we should look at Marx's treatment of economic forms. There is in Marx a theory of how the different symbolic systems of a society are unified and connected in such a way as to produce a single mode of production.

Goux holds that there is present in Marx's analysis of the labor theory of value a general logic of the symbolization process. Marx's whole argument, Goux stresses, is that a purely economic reading of value fails to understand the mechanism of fetishism and the commodity-form. If such a general logic of symbolization can be found in the presentation of Marx on value and money, it then can be examined, Goux argues, in relationship to the genesis of both writing and sexuality. Goux proposes that we approach the genesis of law, religion, or philosophy in the same way that Marx dealt with the genesis of money or the commodity-form in *Capital*. "Our thesis is that in conceptually reproducing the development of contradictions contained in simple exchange . . . Marx discovered a *dialectical logic* that holds for other types of exchange besides market exchange. . . . It is possible to realize, in broad lines, a similar dialectical logic for all sorts of exchanges. . . . On the condition that the category of exchange (and therefore also that of exchange *value*) is given an enlarged, multilateral and complex content. . . . in all social practices; whether these practices are material or signifying there are economic, political, moral, religious, philosophical, aesthetic, sexual and intersubjective aspects of exchange."[21]

If the economy is fundamentally part of a logic of symbolization, then the only manner in which it can be linked with such phenomena as law and religion is through a study of these phenomena at the level of *social forms*. Different practices will be expected, on Goux's model, to share the same form or mode of symbolization as the economy. What Marx called a mode of production is in fact a unification of diverse social practices around a single form or around the reproduction of a single mode of symbolization. Therefore the mode of production should be understood to include not just the production of objects for economic needs but the process of exchange that translates those objects, through symbolic equivalents, into literary, religious, or political meanings.

For Goux each mode of production is also a mode of substitution or exchange. In other words, in every social system there will be specific ways in which objects or persons can be substituted for one another or made equivalent. To make diverse or distinct objects equivalent is an act of meaning. If a society allows so many round metal discs to stand for, or be equivalent to, or be substituted for, a certain quantity of food, that is not due to the *nature* of the objects. Such relations of equivalence emerge because of symbolic systems and therefore are specific to each mode of production. Therefore every society produces its means of subsistence but also produces its own system of exchange. Goux thinks that it is in the systems of exchange or substitution that we will find the link between the economic and the cultural realms. It is in exchange that social form emerges and therefore reveals connections of meaning rather than mechanism.

> Each phase of the genesis of the money-form, which is also
> the development of the forms of value, constitutes . . . the
> form of exchange of a mode of production. This form of
> economic exchange determines, in the last instance, the

mode of substitution in this society, at all levels and in all practices of the social organism. . . . Therefore the mechanistic and positivistic dichotomy between superstructure and base can be made more fluid by grasping the conditions and forms of that metabolism which enters into and constitutes the life of the social organism. In place of dividing the social organism into a movement between a superstructure and a base one grasps its "symbolization" as a whole by considering its dominant "mode of exchange" which intervenes at each level and in each practice.[22]

Goux here emphasizes two themes from cultural anthropology, the study of exchange and the study of social cohesion, or solidarity. Levi-Strauss had pursued in his work the connections between the formation of a social identity in society and the logic by which goods, privileges, women, and stories are exchanged and circulated. Even though the concept of exchange has an economic background, the consequence of Levi-Strauss' approach was that, at least for "primitive" societies, it is impossible to separate clearly economic and cultural forms. For example, Bronislaw Malinowski, in his famous study of the Trobriand Islanders discovered a complex system of exchange of precious objects called the *kula*. This exchange system, however, functioned not as a market, in the form we would recognize today, but as a simultaneous ceremonial, economic, and communicative enterprise.

> The ceremonial exchange of the two articles is the fundamental aspect of the Kula. But associated with it, and done under its cover, we find a great number of secondary activities and features. Thus side by side with the ritual exchange . . . the natives carry an ordinary trade. . . . Further, there are other activities, preliminary to the Kula, or associated with it, such as the building of sea-going canoes, certain forms of mortuary ceremonies and preparatory taboos. The Kula is thus an extremely complex and big institution, both in its geographical extent, and in the manifoldness of its component pursuits. It welds together a considerable number of tribes, and it embraces a vast complex of activities, interconnected, and playing into one another, so as to form an organic whole.[23]

Malinowski was not a follower of Levi-Straussian anthropology, but this particular study illustrates the manner in which a pursuit, whose true outlines and rules remain unknown to the participants, unifies and organizes the entire society. Marx had, of course, stressed such an idea with his concept of totality: A society is not just a collection of activities or persons but a structure or whole which forms and determines its parts. Marx's argument with political economy was partly in terms of the independence that the political economist attributed to market exchange and economic interest. For Marx such activities, including the search for profits, are not given prior to the formation of society but emerge out of it and are inseparable from the whole social fabric of which they form a strand. In this context Marx tends to distinguish between societies in which different social activities are dominant (that is, societies in which ritual rather than economic gain is dominant) and the external condition imposed on every society to produce its means of subsistence. "This much, however, is clear, that the Middle Ages could not live on Catholicism, nor the ancient world on politics. On the contrary, it is the mode in which they gained a livelihood that explains why here politics and there Catholicism, played the chief part."[24]

Malinowski assumes a standard of rational economic activity and therefore measures the primitive rites against this definition of what is "normal." In this fashion the primitive activity, such as the Kula, is seen as an extravagant but nonetheless superfluous way of going about arranging for trade and commerce. It is the sign of a society that lacks utilitarian rationality. Similarly many Marxist thinkers see each activity in society as hiding an economic interest. By externalizing the economic as a separate social activity, traditional Marxism invented a schema of seeing the culture as a mere representation or mirror of economic forces, laws, or interests.

What Goux argues is that to overthrow this utilitarian and economistic tendency within Marxism we must approach the economy as a symbolic system, as a form. Instead of conceiving of the economy as a substratum determining each social practice, or a hidden cause producing visible effects, we should approach it as a mode of substitution or exchange. Once treated in this manner as a form, rather than an interest or law, it can be linked to a general mode of symbolization dominant in the society. Therefore the culture is not produced by some mysterious economic force, but still the culture does correspond to the mode of production. Correspondence, however, is now understood symbolically and not mechanically. A society is a totality not through causal connections but through relationships or meaning and form which we find in the exchange of goods, the rules for sexuality, and systems of expression and communication. "Correspondence is only intelligible if it is emphasized that these two types of exchange, the economic and the semiological (writing, inscriptions and signs) present the same *mode of symbolization.* The concept of 'symbolization' and 'forms of the symbolization process' furnish a concept of the mode of exchange or substitution. . . . In this way the notion of mode of symbolization leads to an enrichment of historical materialism because a close link can be drawn between diverse social practices without utilizing a mechanistic type of causality."[25]

How does Goux intend to use this "dialectical logic" in connecting the economy and the realm of the symbolic? Let us look at the way in which he approaches Marx and Freud. Goux claims to outline a relationship between Freud's theory of human sexuality and Marx's theory of modes of production. Goux does not relate these two thinkers in what has become a traditional manner. Therefore before examining his treatment it might be valuable to review briefly the reasons that have led different social theorists to combine Marx and Freud.

Freud had attempted, after having arrived at his general theoretical and therapeutic positions, to extrapolate his results into a philosophy of culture. He felt that from individual case studies one would find patterns that held for the evolution of the human species as a whole. Therefore concepts such as repression, sublimation, and superego, which Freud had worked out in his topological approach to the mind, were given simultaneously a cultural and a historical meaning. For example, Freud spoke of labor or art as being sublimations on a mass social scale and described the institutions of education, police and the state as embodiments of the human superego. Since Freud wanted to explain morality and religion as complex psychoanalytic processes, it was not difficult to conclude that whole cultures or civilizations could exhibit neurotic symptoms.

Freud's conclusions about culture were pessimistic. While viewing culture as a form of adaptation and sublimation of libidinal energy, Freud stressed that there was an enormous cost of repression, self-denial, and increased aggression for the advances of culture. Repression is demanded by culture since culture is built on the unpleasurable activity of labor, deferred gratification, and obedience to moral codes. Human life in society, Freud concluded, is fundamentally unhappy or discontent, and lack of satisfaction varies directly with the degree of security and stability. The contribution of culture, Freud argued, was that through organized sublimation individuals could form more diverse and complex lives and engage in such highly refined pleasures as art, science, and literature.

In spite of his pessimism there are connections between Marx and Freud in their accounts of culture. Freud had recognized the role of labor and material necessity in the formation of culture and had placed between humanity and nature the technical power of social production. Freud also perceived, as we have seen in Marx, that human needs and desires were changed by the emergence of a complex culture; therefore human nature was the product rather than the origin of social life. But even on this point the differences between Marx and Freud are radical. Freud ultimately held that something like human nature, or a psychological substratum, was at the root of unhappiness in society and would not disappear with even widespread social change. In *Civilization and Its Discontents* Freud expressed a sympathy with socialist struggle for an equal distribution of wealth, but he concluded that socialism rested on a "unscientific" view of human nature which believed that a harmonious community could be created with the given psychological structures of modern humanity.

I have already briefly mentioned Weber's study on Protestantism that suggests some historical corroboration for Freud's insight into the connections between religion, morality, repression of sexuality, and the work ethic. The undoubted application of Freud's work to Victorian social analysis and its extension into problems of disciplining the work force have lead theorists to an amalgam of psychoanalysis with Marxist-style criticism of early capitalism. However, even where the connection between Marx and Freud is sought at a theoretical rather than historical level, as in the work of Herbert Marcuse, it is still based on Freud's works on civilization, culture, and anthropology. Goux, on the other hand, conceives of a quite different relationship between these two thinkers. Goux restricts his attention to Freud's purely psychoanalytic writings, specifically the very early *Three Essays on Sexuality*. Without even going into Freud's works on civilization, Goux wants to show that there are symbolic or "formal" structural similarities between the theories of Marx and Freud. "If one can claim, as it is the object of this book to do, that the 'psychic apparatus' . . . has the same structure as the history of writing, reconstructed on the basis of the history of modes of production and exchange, it is to stress these two aspects. On the one hand, the succession of different phases of the libido . . . but, on the other hand, that the social actualization of these phases depends on the *dominant signifying forms* with which the subject accommodates in reality, forms which result from an historic process presupposed in the social structure."[26] Goux is arguing that there is a relationship between the formation of the economy and the formation of human sexuality because they share a symbolization process rather than a particular institutional or historical link.

Goux bases a great deal of his analysis on constructing an analogy between Marx's presentation of the money-form in *Capital* and Freud's stages of sexuality. There have often been attempts to do a psychoanalysis of money, but Goux is looking at this relationship in purely structural terms as an analogy in the two theories and not the content or fact apparently referred to in the theories.

I have already dealt in this chapter with Marx's treatment of exchange in *Capital*. As we saw, exchange begins with the simple act of barter in its unsystematic and immediate form. Marx claims this is superseded by limited exchange in which objects are traded or bartered against some particular or privileged object (such as a totem). Marx argued that under those conditions the economy of a society is still inseparable from noneconomic forces such as kinship or religion, and it is only with the development of generalized exchange or money that the economy begins to become an autonomous sphere. Objects are exchanged not against "privileges" but in a purely quantitative measure of equal exchange. The ultimate extension of this quantification is money and the emergence of the commodity.

Goux hopes to convince us that there are significant links between Marx's presentation of this history and Freud's account of human sexuality. In a purely syntactic fashion Goux points out that the Freudian oral stage of human development is structurally similar to Marx's simple barter society. If we view the development of sexuality as "symbolically" a system of exchange, then the oral stage represents immediate identification between need and object and therefore no abstract or systematic exchange. In Freud, as is well known, orality is followed by the anal stage in which the child begins to displace desire. A chain of objects such as breast, thumb, pacifier, blanket are linked through identifications in the child's emerging sense of self. For Freud the child must be able to break through to the next stage in which the symbolic object behind all these equivalent exchanges is discovered. Of course the symbolic object is the phallus (at least in Freud's early theory of sexual development), and it allows the child to react not just to partial objects but to desire as a whole and therefore to form a mature self-identity and love object. Goux wants to stress that in both Marx and Freud there seems to be a parallel account of how exchange moves from immediate identity of objects to a system which is explicitly seen as a system of exchange and in which the objects themselves are less important than the symbolic, structural, or formal properties of the system.

> That Marx discovers historically and logically *four phases* in the genesis of the money-form and that Freud is led to distinguish *four stages* in the development of sexual organization is not the result of an accident. . . . It is a similar genetic process, it is the same principle of discontinuous and progressive structuration which commands the ascension to normative sovereignty of gold, the father and the phallus. The phallus is the general equivalent of *objects*, the father the general equivalent of *subjects*, in the same way that gold is the general equivalent of *products*. The elements constituting these wholes are different, but the *syntax* by which one of these elements . . . comes to power and rules the evolution of the whole in which it is excluded is identical.[27]

Our summary of Freud is, of course, very inadequate, but our interest is entirely in Goux's account of the relationship between economic and symbolic structures. Therefore, even without the detail of a full explication, Goux's approach has these aspects. Between the theory of Marx and Freud there is an internal theoretical connection at the symbolic or syntactic level. In Marx's account of money and Freud's account of sexuality we are looking at two identical theories of exchange and object forms. What Marx and Freud shared, Goux concludes, is a general theory of modes of symbolization. For Goux, when a theorist proposes a historical link between, for example, the anal retentive character formation and political control over the labor process, that is in fact only possible because of this more fundamental syntactical link between the two theories.

Goux's emphasis on syntax and sign systems leads him to what could be called a "semiotic objectivism" or a semiotic idealism. Goux seems to be arguing that historical or empirical connections between phenomena such as economic systems, sexual stages of development, and forms of literature are in fact already provided for by the purely structural aspects of systems as a whole—what Goux calls the "modes of symbolization" which all these systems share. For Goux the connection between Marx and Freud is that libido in Freud and labor in Marx can both be reduced to the same function in the two theories. Therefore labor and libido have the same syntax in the two theories and together express the underlying reality of social life. "It is clear that this process described in the field of political economy finds an exact homology in the field of language and writing. The opposition between signified and signifier is nothing other than . . . the split between use value and exchange value. . . . In a precise and limited fashion, through the constant of a parallel hegemony between linguistic meaning and the exchange value of commodities we trace out the contours and decisive implications that this homology suggests."[28]

The claim here is that use value and exchange value in Marx is homologous to the distinction in linguistics between signifier and signified. There are, therefore, some syntactical or formal reasons why theories reach these same distinctions or forms. Goux claims that we can develop a common vocabulary for analyzing different theories and showing their similarities. These similarities translate then into a general logic of symbolization.

Goux wants to claim that a process of symbolization unites labor, libido, and language in human reality and that this symbolic relation is more fundamental and more determining than specified empirical and historical relationships. Is the same "symbolization" found in Freud's theory of sexuality and Marx's genesis of money, or are the theories merely vaguely similar? My question does not imply that one does not expect a connection between economy and psychology. Certainly Freud believed that the hoarding of money and hard labor would ultimately have a psychological explanation. Conversely Marx thought that individual psychological characteristics such as egoistic self-interest would give way to a social and historical analysis. But Goux has gone beyond this and tried to show that these connections are internal to the organization of Marx's theory. Goux is arguing that even before historical research, in the manner of Weber's study, we can discover in the logic of symbolization a pure theoretical necessity. For example, take Goux's comment on the connection between money and sexuality: "Thus, in a general fashion, it is not money as empirical reality nor as unconscious and neurotic signifier which will correspond isomorphically to the phallus. It is the monetary function in the organization of economic exchange and the function of the phallus in the instinctual system of exchange."[29]

By rejecting empirical reality Goux places his theoretical emphasis on the position these terms occupy in the theories. In other words money and the phallus occupy the same symbolic or syntactic position in the monetary and sexual systems of exchange. What Goux is claiming is that we could know through a purely syntactic analysis of the structure of theory the compatibility between a sexual exchange system and an economic exchange system. However, this claim grossly underestimates the complexity of social structures. If you take capitalism as a mode of production, there does not seem to be any way in which to predict what psychological structures will be compatible with it. Early capitalism could be analyzed using the traditional Freudian model of a repressed character structure, but it seems that late capitalism is generating new unrepressed syndromes such as narcissism and hedonism.

The point is that rather than treating Marx and Freud as theoretical schemata or abstractions of more complex and ultimately indeterminate historical developments, Goux approaches history as though it were ruled by some hidden logic or symbolic structure. Goux's semiotic objectivism expresses itself in the imposition onto societies of "laws of symbolization" derived purely from theory which claim to predetermine the movement of history. "The movement of history is the evolution of the total social organism toward its arrangement, at all levels, by the principle of general equivalence. History reaches its summit (we do not say its end) as reorganized and confirmed by the hegemony of major symbols established by the reign of the general equivalent. . . . The summit of history has a place. It comes about with the mode of production founded on monetary exchange and the aftereffect of this summit is history as a science."[30]

Goux's position represents the classical form of historicism. Knowledge of history is itself a condition of history, and therefore history is ruled by some hidden meaning or logic which ultimately brings about its truth as a process. The use of the term science and the attempt to generate connections between events purely in theory, rather than treating them as indeterminate or contingent events, leads Goux to a dogmatic and infallible model of knowledge. Goux attempts to construct a formal synthesis rather than taking theories as a framework for investigation. What emerges is not a theory of society but a metaphysics of social evolution ruled by the pure logic of symbolization.

Goux, influenced like many by Levi-Strauss and his method, is led far beyond a legitimate area of application. It was a brilliant insight on the part of Levi-Strauss to approach society as a system of exchange and extend that to areas such as kinship or mythology. In so doing he opened up fruitful avenues for research in primitive economy since exchange is, of course, a central economic concept. But one cannot leap from such an insight into a single system of signs ruling all society and history. There is a great difference between a theory providing a framework for research, as I claim Marx's theory of labor does, and a metaphysical reduction making research unnecessary and impossible. There is every reason to argue, as I will explore in Baudrillard in the next chapter, that semiology, in its objectivism, determinism, and naturalism, so clearly visible in the hands of Goux, plays an ideological role in the social sciences similar to that of political economy in Marx's time.

3. Objects and Utility

Goux has made, as discussed in chapter 2, a partial deconstruction of the superstructure/base model by arguing that all levels of the social structure reproduce the value-form. He implies then that the economy expresses itself in a symbolic form, and therefore the rest of the social structure does not stand in a phenomenal relation to the economic essence. In this fashion Goux can overcome a type of economism by treating labor (and sexuality or libido) as a syntactic function. We have seen that this reductionism (or universal determinism of the sign) leads to an objectivistic historicism in which the symbolic acts as a logic of history in the Hegelian idealist's sense. In trying to systematize Marx's theory in this manner, Goux produces an objectivism not in the form of deterministic laws of the economy but rather in the manner of Levi-Strauss' naturalistic account of mind and symbolism.

Jean Baudrillard's work is of critical importance in this context since he focuses on Marxism and semiology. In his main theoretical work, *Pour une critique de l' économie politique du signe*, Baudrillard approaches the theory of signs from the position of Marx's critique of commodity fetishism, but he is led into a much deeper reading of Marx's theory of value than we find in Goux.

In an earlier work entitled *The Mirror of Production*, Baudrillard argued that Marx's theory is bound together with classical political economy because Marx accepts the primacy of production.[1] Consequently there is the characteristic falsification of pre-capitalist societies and unexamined assumption of natural needs and utilities underlying Marx's theory of history as there was for classical political economy. "Marx shattered the fiction of *Homo economicus*, the myth which sums up the whole process of the naturalization of the system of exchange value, the market and surplus value and its forms. But he did so in the name of labor power's emergence in action, of man's own power to give rise to value by his labor. Isn't this a similar fiction, a similar naturalization—another wholly arbitary convention, a simulation model bound to *code* all human material and . . . desire . . .?"[2]

Marx's critique of political economy remains incomplete. By accepting some of its fundamental principles—the expression of human needs through use value, the exclusive definition of man through labor, and instrumental relation to nature—Marx internalized, apart from his criticism, the productivist ideal of the age of political economy. For this reason he tends to treat the liberation of the productive forces as synonymous with the liberation of humanity. Such a traditional Enlightenment view of progress proceeds, in part, from Marx's failure to realize that political economy does not only define labor solely from the determination of value but makes labor-power identical to human potential. In Baudrillard we are finally at a historical vantage point which can see the folly of these assumptions, and at the theoretical level we can now show how the conversion of objects into commodities presupposes a relation to human needs, desires, and expressions that is perfectly compatible with the myth of productivism. Marx's naturalistic weak link is now apparent since we can understand, in Baudrillard's sense, the kind of exchanges and needs that are incompatible with commodity production.

Baudrillard uses the concept of the symbolic and symbolic exchange in a way which is radically different from its use by Levi-Strauss. For Baudrillard the symbolic is a critical dimension of demystification, an ever present threat and opposition to the homogeneity of exchange and the commodity-form. The entire social structure mobilizes itself against the non-equivalence, ambivalence, and incommensurability of true symbolic exchange, according to Baudrillard. The concept of symbolic exchange, as a contrast with the socially legitimized appearance of equal exchange, is thus a reformulation of Marx's theory of fetishism. The reformulation of Marx's critique of political economy is the central focus of Baudrillard's work.

As the title of Baudrillard's book suggests, he is drawing a comparison between Marx's critique of political economy through the distinction between use value and exchange value and a critique of semiology that starts from the distinction of the sign into the signifier (the material vehicle of the sign) and the signified (the meaning or concept referred to by the sign). We are to understand the connection as follows: exchange value and signifier designate *relational* forms; use value and the signified stand for the *content* or object of the relations. Here Baudrillard begins with the crucial aspect of mystification or falsity *produced* by the commodity form and extends it to the broader areas of exchange, i.e., discourse and sexuality. It is the mystifying aspect of form that Goux makes positive in an objective history of forms (resulting in his isomorphic parallels between the commodity-form, the sign-form, and the phallic-form). Baudrillard, in opposition, develops the critical side of the term *form*:

> Marx had shown that the objectivity of material production resides not in its materiality but in its *form*. That is the point of departure for all critical theory. The same analytic reduction must be made of ideology: its objectivity does not reside in its "ideality," i.e., in a realist metaphysics of *thought contents*, but in its form. . . . Ideology is in fact the whole process of reduction and abstraction of symbolic material in a form—but the reductive abstraction presents itself immediately as value (autonomy), as content (transcendence), as representation of consciousness (signified). It is the same process that inscribes [*donne à lire*] in the commodity an autonomous value, a transcendent reality, by miscomprehending [*méconnaissance*] its form and the abstract labor that it brings about.[3]

Baudrillard argues that this connection between the commodity-form and the signs leads to the uncovering of a latent idealist anthropology of needs in Marx. Such an anthropology is contained in Marx's naturalization of use value in the labor theory of value of *Capital*. In Baudrillard's language Marx's treatment of use value is as if "the fetishized commodity appears as a real immediate value, correlated with the subject by needs and use value, and circulating according to the rules of exchange value." To correct this limitation of the theory of fetishism only to exchange value, it must be extended from the commodity-form to the realm of the *object-form* (for example, *utility* as a coding of the object prior to exchange).[4] Objects are not autonomous contents waiting to be signified and given a meaning; rather they are, as objects, already coded and formed. Utility already forms the object prior to its exchange. Therefore it cannot be the case that use value refers to a permanent need served by objects. Use value is the *form* in which objects and needs coincide, presupposed in the production of value.

By showing that the value/form is preceded by an object/form,

Objects and Utility 47

Baudrillard can establish a relation between culture and economy without recourse to the model of infrastructure and superstructure. In other words, the production of both objects (as objects of use) and meanings (as in the realm of culture) are related because of their *form*. But in recognizing this we must treat semiology (the study of the production of signs and meanings) as Marx treated political economy. Semiology is the political economy of cultural production, and the sign is the corollary to the commodity. The sign/form and the commodity/form operate through equivalence, reduction, and abstraction.

> Ideology is the very form itself which traverses all the fields of social production. It is the taking up of all production (material or symbolic) in a similar process of abstraction, of reduction, general equivalence and exploitation.
> 1. This is so because *the logic of the commodity and of political economy is at the very heart of the sign* . . . which can function as exchange value (the discourse of communication) and as use value (the rational decoding and social distinctive use of the sign).
> 2. This is so because *the structure of the sign is at its very heart the commodity/form* . . . because it constitutes itself by its form, as a total medium, as a system of communication regulating the whole social exchange. As a form/sign the commodity is a *code* ordering the exchange of value.[5]

Thus Baudrillard aims to show how the commodity/form can extend itself throughout the entire social field with neither a direct theory of causation (economism) nor a representational theory of reflection between superstructure and base. Such a separation between the cultural and the economic is itself a function of the object/form. It is no longer production of the commodity/form as value but the consuming of the objective/form as utility that produces the most intense mystification and social control (hence the shift from political economy to semiology as the subject matter for radical criticism). Furthermore in coding objects for consumption, need, and fulfillment, a new surplus is extracted in the form and level of consumption. If there is exploitation and fetishization at the level of signification, it can only be opposed, according to Baudrillard, with a new form of exchange (exchange which is ambivalent, nonequivalent, nonreductive, and symbolic). Symbolic exchange strikes at the authority of the code.

Thus there is a conjuncture between Baudrillard's rejection of production or labor as the starting point for Marxist theory and his position that political struggles must center on forms of consumption. Before we pursue this, however, a clarification of Baudrillard's critique of Marx is necessary.

The issue revolves around Marx's use of the category "use value" in the treatment of the labor theory of value. Baudrillard claims that Marx imports into the concept of use value an ideology of primary given needs that rests on an assumed autonomous relation of humans to their products. Such a primitive conception of need (and satisfaction) forms the basis of an anthropological objectivism latent in Marx's theory. Baudrillard supports this by quoting those passages early in volume 1 of *Capital* where Marx speaks of use values as constant in all societies or as representing the physiological constant of useful labor. The conclusion seems to be that a use value refers to an object satisfying a need or use directly, whether or not exchange exists, and as a seemingly natural physiological act.[6]

It would appear that, unlike his treatment of exchange value, use value for Marx does not entail the objectification or fetishization of social relations. Implicitly this leads Marx, Baudrillard argues, to assume a *constant of utility*. But then Marx is falsifying and reifying a *form* as though it were a natural property of the object. The assumption that objects are objectively and universally useful circumscribes the whole presentation of labor in a fictitious substratum of human needs.

> It appears that the fetishism of commodities . . . does not operate on the commodity simultaneously as exchange value *and* use value, but only on exchange value. Use value in this restrictive analysis of fetishism does not appear as a social relation, nor therefore as a place of fetishization: utility *as such* escapes the historical determination of class: it designates a final objective relation of simple destination which does not mask itself and whose transparence as *form* defines history (even if its content continually changes with social and cultural determinations). It is here that Marxist idealism operates, it is here that it is necessary to be more logical than Marx himself, in his own sense, more radical. Use value, utility itself, as all abstract equivalence of commodities, is a fetishized *social relation*—an abstraction, that of the *system* of needs, which takes as its

evidence a false concrete destination, a finality proper to
goods and products—just as the abstraction of social labor
which grounds the logic of equivalence (exchange value)
hides itself under the illusion of value infused in the commodity.[7]

Marx's famous quote concerning the "different hunger" satisfied by
knife and fork rather than by tearing meat off a bone is not an answer
to Baudrillard's criticism. Such a view simply assumes change in content due to cultural relativity while preserving an unmediated relationship to the satisfaction of the need *as need*, i.e., as object/form.
According to Baudrillard, then, even in that quote Marx still assumes
that *the object's* usefulness or ability to satisfy a human need is somehow naturally there and given rather than formed through social relations. Marx never entertains the problem of a *system of needs* (or
needs as a social form) as he does with the commodity. Marx asserts in
Capital that use values, unlike exchange values, are "incomparable"
and their irreducible particularity makes it impossible to treat them in
a homogeneous fashion. However, Baudrillard's approach stresses the
homogeneous function of use value. For there to be exchange value it
is already necessary that *utility* become the principle of reality for the
object as product. Exchange presupposes that the objects are already
rationalized as useful. The reduction to utility is the basis for both
exchange and systematization and the precondition, in Baudrillard, for
fetishism (which he defines as the reduction of the symbolic-ambiva-
lent to the systematic-equivalent). For Baudrillard, exchange and the
equivalence-form are made possible by an object's becoming comparable through the common denominator of functional/rational. (Only
the objects of symbolic exchange retain their true singularity and incommensurability.) Therefore, to be more radical than Marx is to see
the priority of the object/form over the commodity/form.

Every object is translatable in the abstract general code of
utility, which is its reason, its objective law, its
meaning. . . . It is functionality which enters the object as
code, and this code, which bases itself on the adequacy of
an object to its end (use), surmounts all real and virtual objects. . . . The commodity/form is only the developed form
of this economic calculus to which it continually returns.
But the use value (utility) is also a *social relation*, contrary
to the anthropological illusion which wants to create a

simple relation between the "need" of man and the usefulness of the object. Just as in exchange value the man/producer does not appear as the creator but only as socially abstract labor power, so in the system of use values the man/consumer never appears as desire and fulfillment [*jouissance*] but as socially abstract need power.[8]

With the rationalization of utility as the condition for the equivalence form (and the consequent exploitation centered on the functional object/form instead of the economic value/form), we now see that social domination is outside the direct laboring process and cultural manipulation of needs takes on a new political significance. The latent fetishizing of use value, as already found in Marx, reappears throughout Marxism in the failure to grasp the significance of consumption as autonomous from production.[9]

There are two sides to Baudrillard's reading of Marx. First, Baudrillard argues that the priority Marx gives to labor (*and to praxis*) binds his theory to the very sphere Marx criticizes—namely, political economy. Even though Marx uses labor as a philosophical concept encompassing human activity, it is precisely such an assumption that is the object of Baudrillard's analysis. "The system of political economy does not produce only the individual as labor power that is sold and exchanged: it produces the very conception of labor power as the fundamental human potential."[10]

Second, Baudrillard explicitly rejects what Goux called the dialectical mode of presentation. Baudrillard sees the dialectical method and the concept of labor as inextricably bound together. Therefore he shows that if we are to question seriously the model of superstructure and base, we must reject in turn the heritage of Hegelianism that Marx accepted in defending his position on production and exchange. To understand this point we must consider what Marx called the dialectical or abstract-concrete method.

Marx described the method of *Capital* as one of moving from the abstract to the concrete in presenting a total picture of society. In other words, he stressed that the reader would find in *Capital* neither a straight historical narrative nor a haphazard collection of concepts. The beginning point of the commodity is not arbitrary, however, even though it does not refer to an actual historical beginning point. The commodity represents in a condensed form the whole of modern society. The commodity is like an essence that captures the whole.

Objects and Utility 51

Therefore Marx's presentation moves the reader from seeing the commodity as an object to seeing it as a social relation. In so doing the context or social structures that stand behind and are hidden by the "thinglike" objectivity of the simple objects exchanged in the market must be filled in.

Baudrillard believes that Marx is misled by this model of presentation borrowed from Hegel. But if we consider what Marx has said, then it is significant that the comments about use value occur in the first sections of *Capital*. According to Marx it would be an incorrect reading to leap to the conclusion that use value refers to a permanent or natural quality of things. In following his method, Marx, contrary to what Baudrillard concludes, seems to refer consciously to the natural or physical aspects of objects as a *form*. Therefore we could interpret the notion of natural or immediate, when applied to the concept of use value, as a reference to its place in the demonstration of *Capital*. The terms *natural* and *immediate* do not refer to a fixed need, as in the quote, but to the form of appearance of objects.

> Therefore they only appear as commodities, or have the form of commodities insofar as they possess a *double form*, i.e., natural form and value form.
> This contradiction can be overcome by objectifying it, i.e., by positing the commodity as a *double form*, first in its *natural immediate form*, then in its mediated form, as money.

But in fact Baudrillard's argument goes further than this specific theoretical point. Baudrillard primarily points to passages where Marx speaks of a "metabolism between man and nature" or the everlasting "imposed necessity" of labor.[13] Isn't it apparent, Baudrillard argues, that Marx conceives of history within certain fixed, immutable needs? That would be the case if Marx meant by labor only utilitarian or purely economic activity. If Marx really did share the assumption of political economy, then the production of exchange value would be the eternal form of labor. But I have already argued at length that we do not need to read Marx as an economic determinist.

The "imposed necessity" that Marx speaks of in terms of labor is not its ability to produce use values but the recognition that human needs, as well as objects, are produced. Marx is arguing against a view of naturally given needs and in defense of a view of needs as socially mediated. This passage from the *Grundrisse* makes exactly that point in terms of the constant aspect of labor. Baudrillard is simply incorrect to view the constancy in Marx as one of needs or objects (as objects of use). Marx seems to make clear that he regards both needs and objects as social. "The object is not the only thing which production creates for consumption. Production also gives consumption its specificity. . . .the object is not the object in general, but a specific object which must be consumed in a specific manner, to be mediated in its turn by production itself."[14]

Marx's intention is to weaken the labor theory of political economy by showing its historical limitations. Certainly for Marx, as for Baudrillard, there are forms of labor and exchange which are not reducible to the opposition of exchange and use value. Marx's position is that if need and labor are historical, then society is not based on any natural or biological cause but in fact produces, along with its means of subsistence, its subjects, objects, and needs.

Every society will attempt to present its form of social life as a natural necessity. In capitalism the fetishism of the commodity/form acts to create an identity between the natural and social qualities of things and therefore reifies the labor process within the production of surplus value.

At this point Marx sounds exactly like Baudrillard. The criticism is at root identical, and Baudrillard agrees that Marx's analysis of exchange is a model for critical social theory. Therefore the real point of difference is not whether Marx adopted some naturalistic assumptions in his theory of use value. The question is whether looking at society through the concept of symbolic exchange rather than labor results in a more comprehensive theory. Baudrillard is quite convincing in rejecting a naturalistic interpretation of Marx, and I totally agree. However, he is not convincing in showing that Marx did not understand use values as social forms or that a theory of labor necessarily entails what Baudrillard calls an "anthropologism of needs."

Baudrillard, influenced by Levi-Strauss and the sociologist-anthropologist Marcel Mauss, has shown what an important role exchange plays in the formation and function of culture. I have already tried to show that Marx also, in his own language, recognized a similar aspect of social phenomena. But since Marx did not adopt a utilitarian account of work there is no need to treat Marx's analysis as opposed to an account of symbolic exchange. Marx's theory of labor excompasses what Baudrillard calls symbolic exchange.

My point can be amplified by looking at what Baudrillard means by the idea of symbolic exchange. For Baudrillard the ideology of utilitarianism and political economy rests on the notion that all objects are basically equivalent since all objects can be reduced to a single standard of economic need. But in every society there are needs and desire that transcend this utility, and that is precisely what he calls symbolic exchange. Symbolic exchange challenges the commodity fetishism in society by expressing the lack or desire that cannot be fulfilled by purely economic production. What does Baudrillard mean by a consumption of objects that is neither utilitarian nor functional in an economic sense? There is evidence that primitive societies exhibit what some anthropologists call "irrational" economic activity. The obvious examples are the potlatch ceremonies, where surplus goods are destroyed, or the famous exchange network of the Trobriand Islanders studied by Malinowski.

For the moment we may assume that examples of gift giving and gratuitous exchange or consumption would at least approximate Baudrillard's idea of a symbolic (versus an economic) act of exchange. Having established such a category why does Baudrillard consider it so important? Apparently symbolic exchange is the only aspect of social life that continues to resist the integration of social life into the market economy. Society has the power to mold subjects through the object/forms it makes available to satisfy our needs and desires. Such is the material basis of what Marx called, in the realm of philosophy, ideology. Marx thought that we could save ourselves from the crushing anarchism of the market by emancipating the laboring class from wages and private ownership of factories. For Baudrillard such a strategy is no longer enough. The commodity now goes further than the economy. It has become a sign that codes and forms our acts of communication and consumption. Exploitation does not occur any longer only in factories among workers; it is now extended into the whole cultural realm where all desires are channeled into what is functional, useful, or equivalent to the needs produced by the society. The culmination of this extension is a proliferation of objects whose purpose is not to satisfy needs but to create and simultaneously fill those needs which are compatible with and integrated into the social order.

For Baudrillard, need and satisfaction are a circle by which consumption integrates any demand into its social equivalents. The object/form is then both a commodity and a sign. It is both economic and cultural. As a commodity an object sublimates all social need into ownership and consumption. As a sign the object abolishes any symbolic or ambivalent (that is, nonequivalent) qualities of exchange. The exploitation of labor, which Marx described, is only possible, Baudrillard argues, because human desire is already imprisoned within the utilitarian and functional model of humanity. Not only did Marx not appreciate this more important symbolic level, Baudrillard continues, but he was himself seduced by the utilitarian aspects of political economy. Baudrillard could well agree with this rejection of a "dialectic of production" by the philosopher Michael Foucault. "The twentieth century will undoubtedly have discovered the related categories of exhaustion, excess, the limit and transgression—the strange and unyielding form of these irrevocable movements which consume and consummate us. In the form of thought which considers man as worker and producer . . . consumption was based entirely on need and need based itself exclusively on the model of hunger. . . . it inserted man into a dialectic of production which had a single anthropological meaning; if man was alienated from his real nature and immediate needs through his labor and the production of objects with his hands, it was nevertheless through its agency that he recaptured his essence and achieved the indefinite gratification of his needs."[15]

Therefore not only the nineteenth-century model of production and need but also the nineteenth-century model of social change is obsolete. It is not the workings of economic laws or the market that will bring about a crisis. Marx believed that capitalism would end through a combination of economic crisis and political organization of the working class. Baudrillard offers only the ultimate exhaustion of consumption. Baudrillard reminds us that symbolic demand is characterized by the fact that it is unfulfilled and cannot be met by the logic of value and utility. In the commodity any demand of the subject is supposed to be completely sublimated into objects. "But behind the sublimation of value there is something irreducible; sometimes it takes the form of violent destruction, but more often it takes the concealed form of deficit, exhaustion and a refusal or resistance to both the investment and fulfillment of desire . . . which takes the form of what could be called the tendency of the rate of pleasure [*jouissance*] to fall."[16]

What Baudrillard has said is that instead of there being a purely economic breakdown in modern society, there will be a subjective exhaustion of the consumer. Resistance will emerge against needs being translated into commodities or preformed objects. Resistance will be in the form of not finding fulfillment through consumption rather than in human working conditions. The rate and intensity of consumption will have to be continually raised to achieve even a limited amount of enjoyment. Baudrillard therefore places emphasis on the aesthetic or subjective aspects of the object/form and its connection with crisis through exhaustion. He wants to show that the economic system has no purely objective limitations in the sense that Marx hoped to discover. The weak point of the economy is rather precisely its attempt to regulate all of human exchanges solely through the production of objects which are consumed in the satisfaction of needs.

There are aspects of Baudrillard's position that echo an old tradition in political philosophy. Before Marx the various critical theories of capitalist development tended to be found in German Romanticism and what was later called French Utopian socialism. In both of these cases the arguments tended to concern qualitative objections to the market economy. Resistance to capitalism and its effects on life were primarily to its aesthetic and subjective impact. Social theory tended to reject capitalism under the broad heading of industrialization and revived a nostalgia for a simpler, more agricultural mode of life. The problem of alienation made its appearance during this period but in the broad sense of divisions between nature and culture or man's sensuous and rational sides. Marx took great pains to distinguish himself from such views, which may explain his persistent emphasis on an objective and lawful analysis of capitalism. Marx believed that such criticism of capitalism, which rejected industrial development as a whole, would make it impossible for human life to reap the benefits of capitalist expansion. For that reason *The Communist Manifesto* begins with a lengthy hymn of praise for the improvements brought about by capitalism which Marx says revolutionized the means of production. Marx then ends his discussion by criticizing utopian socialism in its different forms.

I am not suggesting that Baudrillard's position is the same as utopian socialism at Marx's time. But Baudrillard has not fully considered Marx's views about production in their strongest form. First of all it is unlikely that Marx envisioned anything like an automatic breakdown of capitalism. Economic crisis is not a simple lawful or objective process of necessity. But Marx certainly held that it isn't wholly wrong to talk of capitalist expansion reaching its limits. These limits, whether they are experienced as lack or exhaustion by the members of society, do still have independent consequences.

But we need not go into the complicated question of economic crises. The second problem with Baudrillard's criticism of Marx is more central. Baudrillard places symbolic demand rather than labor at the center of resistance in society. But there is a strong argument, in Marx's own presentation, that a commodity-producing society would be strengthened rather than weakened by the experiences of "demand" or lack of fulfilment. As Marx showed, the commodity-form supplies not simply food, shelter, and clothing but complex needs of social status, self-identity, and cultural hegemony. Are not feelings of exhaustion and lack the very thing on which to base a consumer society?

Baudrillard seems to underestimate the very powerful social order he describes. To offer the hope of exhaustion against the massive integration of our culture and economy under the single code of the commodity is no different than the traditional Marxist hope that capitalism will suddenly collapse.

Baudrillard has a penetrating criticism of certain assumptions within Marxism and the manipulative attitude built into modern socialist societies. For Baudrillard modern socialism is continuing exploitation because it naïvely assumes that exploitation can only occur in the economy. Because socialism is built only to allow its members to satisfy their needs as use values, it perpetuates, in a concealed form, its power over the culture and social relations. "To radically subvert the logic of exchange value it is not sufficient to restore the autonomy of use value, it is necessary to restore the possibility of giving, that is to say to change the form of social relations. . . . In preserving, in spite of their radical analysis, a certain level of value (use value) the so-called liberators have really preserved a certain level of power and manipulation."[17]

We must extend the political struggle to wider spheres of culture and show how the forms that Marx analyzed in economics now operate throughout the culture. But does such an expansion of concern in social theory relegate Marx's concept of labor to oblivion? I don't think that is as obvious as Baudrillard seems to hold. If we must liberate, as Baudrillard says, the relationship of exchange itself (a new form of "giving"), then there must be some action. But activity is precisely what Marx wanted to concentrate on and make the center of social analysis and social change. If Baudrillard claims that a specific object/form precedes, at the symbolic level, the different forms of labor, it still remains that the only way to change such a situation is through the labor that creates the objects. Baudrillard says at one point that we should decide to treat an object as purposeless as a *res nulla*. Certainly this is a radical act, but carried out in isolation it would have little

Objects and Utility 57

impact on the society and probably lead to the demise of its perpetrator. An object freed from the code of utility understood as an object/form is a consequence of abandoning commodity production. It cannot be accomplished, however, before human beings actually stop producing commodities. Baudrillard has shown a great deal about the inner workings of Marx's account of labor. Instead of rejecting what Marx called praxis in society, it now becomes necessary to consider what production and labor would look like if they were not purely economic and utilitarian. Can production and what Baudrillard calls desire be brought together?

4. The Production of Desire

BAUDRILLARD'S main point is that the category of exploitation should be shifted from commodity production to the level of the sign (coding system) where objects for consumption form an equivalence of meaning between needs and desires. The possibility of symbolic exchange, as a noneconomistic form of consumption, fights the fetishization of the object as a use value and as a satisfaction of given needs. Baudrillard concludes that the hegemony of exchange value/use value is not broken through a new form of labor, which still accepts the ideology of production, but through a new form of incommensurable symbolic exchange.

Deleuze and Guattari in their work *L'Anti-Oedipe*, while agreeing with Baudrillard's attack on the representational model of desire, insist on still taking production as the central concept and therefore viewing desire as a form of production.[1] For Deleuze and Guattari desiring production and social production are a continuous process—what they call a flux—and thus they do not begin with the field of semiology (the realm of cultural reproduction) as do Goux and Baudrillard. Deleuze and Guattari can agree with Marx's starting point of material production if it is understood in the broadest metabolic terms. Their analysis attempts to unify a microanalysis at the level of the body with a macroanalysis at the level of social structures and institutions using the notion of desiring machine or desiring production.

The position of *L'Anti-Oedipe* is that "It is at the level of Flux and . . . *not* at the level of ideology, that the integration of desire is brought about."[2] Desire does not belong to the sphere of ideology, i.e., representation or phantasm of reality. Desire is a flux or a flow, not a symbolic simulacrum. Therefore it does not stand in a signified relation to production but squarely within it. In agreement with Baudrillard, Deleuze and Guattari do not see desire as the representation

The Production of Desire

of naturally given needs. But in opposition to Baudrillard neither is desire something rediscovered in moments of nonreciprocal exchange. For Deleuze and Guattari the dominant ideology of modern society is exchangist, that is, it reduces social reproduction to the sphere of circulation. Such a reduction has a double impact. First, it only allows us to see the integration of desire into the social whole at the level of the circulation of goods (for the satisfaction of needs), not at the level of the production of the desire itself. Second, it conceals the link between labor and desire. Desire only appears in the negative sense of lack of fulfillment but not as self-production. The reason Deleuze and Guattari are dissatisfied with Baudrillard's symbolic, nonequivalent form of exchange is that they are trying to develop a more complex view of how production and culture form a whole in different societies. One of the main themes of *L'Anti-Oedipe* is that social structures have different means for controlling the production of both objects and needs. Each society has specific forms which channel need and desire back into the social institutions so as not to allow the emergence of what Baudrillard called ambivalence or nonfulfillment. The main contrast for Deleuze and Guattari is between pre-capitalist societies, which utilize a coding of needs around specific and restricted cultural objects, and capitalism, which allows for expanding production solely regulated by exchange and the accumulation of value. We will explore that contrast.

To be exchanged and to be equivalent is synonymous in modern economics, and it is a logic that leaves no relation or social level untouched. No previous society has been integrated or organized in such a massive fashion. Capitalism has a radical relation to all previous societies since it liberates production from all the boundaries that pre-capitalist societies erect against productive and economic autonomy. Capitalism thrives on the kind of energy which is only possible at the cost of tearing apart the careful controls over activity in pre-capitalist societies. Such a transformation affects not merely the level of goods and money but the forms of human labor and desire.

In one of Marx's explanations of the term *abstract labor*, he shows the connection between productivity as a form of liberation and dominance of the equivalence-form.

> Indifference towards a specific kind of labor presupposes a very developed totality of real kinds of labor, of which no single one is any longer dominant. As a rule, the most gen-

> eral abstractions arise only in the midst of the richest possible concrete development, where one thing appears common to many, to all. Then it ceases to be thinkable in a particular form alone. On the one side, this abstraction of labor as such is merely the mental produce of a concrete totality of labors. Indifference towards specific labors corresponds to a form of society. . . . Not only the category of labor but labor in reality has here become the means of creating wealth in general, and has ceased to be organically linked with particular individuals in any specific form.[3]

Deleuze and Guattari's controversial thesis is that such a process culminates in capitalism's production of schizophrenia. Schizophrenia is the social experience of a total identity and indifference. It is not a disease but the historical breakdown inherent in and haunting this universalization of equivalence and exchange which is the capitalist mode of production. The schizophrenic is a product of absolute decoding and complete desocialization of the body—a descent into indifference and homogeneity. The schizophrenic is the commodity which can no longer enter into the exchange process. Schizophrenia is the true industrial waste offering a weak link, for Deleuze and Guattari, in the capitalist repression of desire.

> The relation of schizophrenia to capitalism goes beyond the problems of mode of life, environment, ideology, etc., and must be posed at the deepest level of a single and same economy, of a single and same process of production. Our society produces schizos like automobiles and shampoo with the only difference that schizos are not saleable. . . . One could say that schizophrenia is the *exterior* limit of capitalism itself or boundary of its most profound tendency. But capitalism can only function on the condition that it inhibits this tendency or represses and displaces this limit by substituting its own relatively *immanent* limits that it endlessly reproduces on an enlarged scale. The Marxist law of a counter-tendency must be reinterpreted in such a manner. . . . The problem for capitalism is to link . . . energy in a world axiomatic which always opposes new interior limits to the revolutionary power of the decoded flux.[4]

Capitalism is a form of society which liberates the subject's productivity from organic, biological, and social boundaries. But it must immediately rechannel this freed production and subjectivity into the equivalence-form (which is a kind of interiorized limit). For *L'Anti-Oedipe* the fuel of capital is the release of subjectivity in the form of production as both labor and desire. But each time the society decodes the subject's identity, it renews a potential threat of nonintegration, namely, that desire will not be able to be channeled through the form of exchange. Schizophrenia as a product of decoding cannot be integrated back into the capitalist axiomatic. "The Flux is decoded and axiomatized simultaneously in capitalism. Therefore schizophrenia (which escapes the axiomatic) is not the identity of capitalism but on the contrary its difference, its disappearance and its death."[5]

The project of *L'Anti-Oedipe* is to understand how different societies control desire and labor. As the title indicates Deleuze and Guattari conclude that the Oedipus complex (and with it the whole psychoanalytic institution with its legal, medical, and industrial forms) is precisely a social force holding our subjectivity within the confines of the institutional form of the family. Human desires find their expression only within familial exchange and therefore their social and productive reality are effectively integrated.

The relation of *L'Anti-Oedipe* to psychoanalysis is actually two-sided. First, Freud made the important discovery of libido, the abstract power of desire, and for Deleuze and Guattari made possible an analysis of desiring production (as libido and as labor). But at the same time psychoanalysis is structured to rechannel libido into the private sphere of the family. Therefore, Freud and psychoanalysis stand in relation to the theory of desire as classical political economy does with regard to a theory of labor. In traditional political economy the discovery of productivity in general (i.e., labor) is accompanied by naturalizing production in its particular historical form. Similarly with desire, the abstraction of desire from its particular manifestation to form the concept of libido is immediately naturalized as familial exchange in Freud. Deleuze and Guattari see both desire and labor as part of subjectivity:

> As Marx says, it is in capitalism that the essence becomes subjective, *productive activity in general*, and that abstract labor becomes something real by which all previous social formations can be re-interpreted from the viewpoint of decoding or a generalized process of deterritorialization. . . .
> It is the same thing with abstract desire as libido, as sub-

jective essence. It is not simply a question of a mere parallel between social capitalist production and desiring production, or even between the capital-money flux and the excrement-flux of desire. The relation is much closer: The desiring machine is nothing more than the social machine, so that the conjuncture of decoded fluxes in the capitalist machine tends to liberate free figures of a universal subjective libido. Briefly, the discovery of a productive activity *in general and without distinction*, such as it appears in capitalism, is inseparable from the discoveries of political economy *and* psychoanalysis. . . . That is not to say that the capitalist man desires labor or that labor follows desire in capitalism. The identity of labor and desire is rather, not a myth, but the active utopia *par excellence* which designates the capitalist limit that desiring production overcomes. But why, precisely, is desiring production finally always antagonistic to capitalism? . . . capitalism, in the same moment that it discovers the subjective essence of desire and labor—the common essence of productive activity in general—immediately alienates it again in a repressive machine which separates and maintains the essence as divided; abstract labor on one side, abstract desire on the other: political economy *and* psychoanalysis, political economy *and* libidinal economy . . . the appearance of psychoanalysis within capitalism.[6]

Deleuze and Guattari demonstrate their thesis in two broad criticisms. First, the Oedipus complex is attacked within psychoanalysis and psychoanalytic theory (as well as therapeutic practice). Here they try, to put it schematically, to recover a radical Freud of the libido theory from the conservative Freud of the metapsychology and Greek mythology. Schizophrenia is the anomaly that always disrupted the psychoanalytic model, and the schizophrenic's refusal to remain enclosed within the familial analysis of Oedipus is not an example of resistance but a basis for a social and materialist theory of desire. The schizophrenic teaches us that, according to Deleuze and Guattari, desire is invested throughout the social field—not primarily within the family—and that desire is something produced rather than representative.

Second, the attack on Oedipus is begun again, in the middle sections of the book, through a history of desiring production as social production. The book is not concerned with whether or not the Oedipus complex exists in all societies but with why the complex appears universal with capitalism. Oedipus is the *form* of desire just as Marx showed that the commodity labor-power is the *form* of labor in a society of generalized exchange and equivalence. Deleuze and Guattari's revision of Marx's theory of history is meant to show how the culture forms the desires and needs of a society as well as it forms social production.

Savagery and Barbarism

The following history of pre-capitalist societies is from the section of *L'Anti-Oedipe* that is most centrally concerned with Marx's theory. I have used this section selectively since my intention is to contrast the position of Deleuze and Guattari with those of the other theorists we have been considering. Again I have taken Marx, Levi-Strauss, and Freud as our central themes concerning the concept of society and exchange.

For the authors the essential point of their work is to show how the concept of production in Marx can be integrated into a broader theoretical framework that includes desire as well as labor. They want to study how a society controls not merely the production and distribution of goods but simultaneously the production and control over desires and needs. Deleuze and Guattari want to show that between capitalism and pre-capitalist societies there is a dramatic shift in the control over social desires and needs that parallels the emergence of a commodity-producing society. The separation between culture and economy created by the introduction of the value-form, a separation Marx expresses in the superstructure-base metaphor, also creates, in Deleuze and Guattari's analysis, a separation between public and private expressions of desire finding their outlet in the dominance of the family in modern social structure. "But the [capitalist] universe has for its function dividing the subjective essence [identity of nature] into two functions, that of alienated abstract labor in private property which reproduces enlarged interior limits for capitalism and that of alienated abstract desire in the privatized family which produces ever narrower interior limits. It is this double alienation of labor and desire which endlessly deepens and enlarges differences inside this essential identity."[7]

The point therefore of a history of desire as production is to show

how societies are organized to contain desire and how differences in that control relate to different forms of subjectivity itself.

When Deleuze and Guattari use the term *coding* in relation to desire, they are referring only to pre-capitalist societies. They divide pre-capitalist social formations broadly into primitive, kinship-based societies (savagery) and regimes of central state power, in which lineage is replaced by a despotic ruler (barbarism). In the primitive society desire and production are unified as the *earth*. Each flux, whether it is a metabolism of procreation, agriculture, exchange, or language, must be coded so that it is inscribed on and does not escape the regulation of the societies' collective source and body—in this case, the earth itself.

The primitive form of the code is writing directly on the body— "tatooing, excising, carving up, sacrificing, mutilating, initiating." In this way each organism is a collective body, an earth on which the social demands are literally written. The code is physically present on both the forces and the agents of the production process. But this code is a weak form of control. It is limited to physical marking and still must contain very complex and qualitatively distinct processes. For example the flux of herds and grain or sperm and menses are to be coded in the same way. The inherent limit is that as there is a growing complexity to population and production (two distinct fluxes), the control and constraint purely through physical marks must be replaced by a more internalized code. "It is an act of foundation, by which man ceases to be a biological organism and becomes a full body, an earth on which are inscribed . . . the demands of the socius. It is a question of giving man a memory: man, who is constituted by an active faculty of forgetting, must *make* for himself another memory, a collective memory, through the repression of biological memory, a memory of speech and no longer of things, a memory of signs and no longer of effects. This terrible alphabet constitutes a system of cruelty whose organization traces the sign on the body itself."[8]

Coding does not allow wealth or prestige to escape collective investment.[9] This is why production in primitive society cannot be treated as a solely economic activity. No activity can become autonomous from the regulation of the social body, since that would be a direct threat to the code. For Deleuze and Guattari, each production process, however, has the potential for abstraction and privatization. But either moment would deny to the regime the collective appropriation of an organ or an activity. In fact, in the primitive society desire appears as that which lies beyond the code (the violation of the interdiction) and therefore is represented by a body which is no longer communal, no longer a collective investment—a body which is not human. "Deterritorialization is the nightmare that the primitive machine wards off with all its forces . . . nightmare or anguished premonition of what will be the decoding of the flux and the collective disinvestment of organs, and being-abstract of the flux of desire and the being-private of organs. . . . The primitive machine does not ignore exchange, commerce and industry, it wards them off, localises them, encases them maintaining the merchant . . . in a subordinated position so that the flux of exchange and production does not come to break the code in the name of abstract and fictive quantities."[10]

From the limits of primitive society we move on to the formation of despotic regimes which replace the lineage-based communal systems with a relatively private relation between the ruler and the subjected masses. The despotic state (here Deleuze and Guattari combine analyses taken from Marx's treatment of Asiatic despotism and Engel's treatment of barbarism) replaces nature or earth with the body of the despot. The despotic ruler is a code which substitutes for the primitive marking on flesh abstract signs (systems of writing, legality, morality, bureaucracy) which create the potential for both property and wealth. It is its centralization over production, as represented abstractly by the body of the despot, that makes such control distinct from the primitive.

> The essence of the State is the creation of a new inscription by which the new body, immobile, monumental and immutable, appropriates all the forces and agents of production; but this inscription allows the older territorial inscriptions to remain. . . . The imperial inscription recovers all the territorial alliances and affiliations and makes them converge on the direct affiliation of the despot with God, the new alliance of the despot with the people. All the coded fluxes of the primitive machine are maintained up to the point where the despotic machine overcodes them. *Overcoding*, which constitutes the essence of the centralized state, is at the same time a measure of its continuity and rupture with ancient formations. There is still the horror of desire which will not be coded but also the establishment of a new inscription which overcodes and makes desire the possession of the despot.[11]

This introduces a new economy of repression. In the primitive social formation there is no direct sign of repression; desire is coded indirectly by coding all activities and not allowing privatization. Now the despot *represents* and stands for repression. Instead of attempting to regulate all activities the people are allowed a private and personal existence as subjects. As in Hegel's analysis of the Roman world, it is the universalization and abstraction of the state that proves to be its despotic authority. Human desire and need itself become direct objects of the code because the code is now the abstraction of legal and moral prohibitions.[12]

Capitalism

There is an enigmatic line of Marx which Deleuze and Guattari take as an essential insight: "World history did not always exist; history as world history is a result."[13] For them this means that capitalism *produces* universality, and thus world history, through its unique function of decoding. It substitutes for the intrinsic coding of pre-capitalist social formations a pure quantification and expansion of production. Abstract labor, for example, is the decoding of previously natural forms of labor. It reveals the *universal* of all societies as generalized productive activity. Capital is a permanent revolt against coding and therefore grasps *in negation* all previous social formations. "In a certain way capitalism has haunted all forms of society, but haunts them as their terrifying nightmare, the panic and fear they have of a flux which will overflow their codes. On the other hand, if it is capitalism which determines the conditions and possibility of universal history, it is only to the extent that it has to do with its own essential limits, its own destruction. . . . Briefly, universal history is not only retrospective, it is contingent, singular, ironic and critical."[14]

As we have seen, the primitive social formation is constantly threatened by the dispersion of its codes. For example, the primitive coding of desire is through a direct marking of the body specifying and qualifying the investment of bodily organs as collective rather than privatized. As a barrier to the privatization of desire it therefore prevents any equivalent exchange. The sense of capitalism as the negation of previous social formations is in its liberation of all productivity and all objects from any such codes (from all intrinsic specificity) in the name of the generalized abstraction of productivity. "It is not primitive societies which are outside of history, it is capitalism which is at the end of history. Capitalism results from a long history of contingencies and accidents which bring about this end but one can say that the previous formations did not preview it. Capitalism has only come externally through the force of arising and being provided for from within."[15]

As was clear from Marx's argument the function of the commodity-form is that it generalizes exchange and equivalence. The commodity institutes a massive deterritorialization for the purposes of intensifying productivity in general. Capital replaces both the earth and the despot as the sources of order since it is *activity*, rather than positive code or limit, that it seeks. As a process, capital centers on the flux of producers and the flux of money, both of which embody productivity per se and therefore allow for its quantification. Abstraction, deterritorialization, privatization, and quantification are all moments in a unified process described in *L'Anti-Oedipe*.

> At the heart of capital Marx demonstrated the coincidence of two principal elements: on the one side the deterritorialized worker, free and naked having to sell his labor-power, and on the other side decoded money becoming capital. . . . each of these elements puts into play several processes of decoding and deterritorialization of the soil by privatisation; decoding of the instrument of production by appropriation; privatisation of the means of consumption by dissolution of familial relations; finally decoding of the worker to the profit of labor itself or the machine—and, for capital, deterritorialization of wealth by monetary abstraction; decoding the flux of producers through market capital; decoding the State through financial capital; decoding of the means of production through the formation of industrial capital.[16]

In the terminology of *L'Anti-Oedipe* capitalism is not a new code for desire or labor. Coding is not inherently economic; rather it determines the *quality* of objects as they pass over the source of social value—goods for consumption, goods for prestige, etc. The code rigorously defines, limits, and separates, and therefore no equivalence is allowed to obliterate each object's unique relation to the community's collective investment. For the primitive society only the code prevents the various circuits of exchange and circulation from becoming wholly dispersed, forming no communal investment. In fact the very possibility of the limit and boundary disappearing is precisely what the primitive social formation protects itself against. It fears the breaking of social prohibitions and restraints.

> All the characteristics of the code, namely that it is indirect, qualitative and limited, show sufficiently that a code is not and cannot be economic; on the contrary it expresses the apparent objective movement in which the economic forces and productive connections are attributed to an extra-economic moment which they emanate from and which serves as a support and agent of inscription. . . . in the case of feudalism, for example, the juridical and political relations are *determined to be dominant* because surplus labor . . . constitutes a qualitatively and temporally distinct flux from that of labor and can only enter into a whole that is itself qualitative and implies non-economic factors.[17]

Within the limits of the code the only exploitation and appropriation possible is through its intensification (overcoding) but not through the act of production. Exploitation is still, as Marx says, separated in both time and space from the activity of labor itself in pre-capitalist societies. Thus to say that capitalism is a liberation of productivity (the flux as labor and desire) is merely to say that both take on the character of abstract equivalents. Exchange therefore has no limits; there is no distinct and qualitative limit resisting generalized exchange. In the form of abstract labor-power, labor appears as productivity which can be set in relations of equivalence to objects and needs. Thus while at one moment human productivity is released in capitalism from all intrinsic barriers (the intrinsic codes of pre-capitalist society), it is still controlled by anonymously reproducing itself only in the commodity-form. Thus the wage laborer is not held to the production of a surplus by the imposition of a code identifying his labor with an extra-economic constraint. On the contrary, in capital the process is wholly immanent since the productivity of labor is made to appear equivalent to the production of commodities. Therefore abstraction and quantification create not a boundary but a coincidence between the laborer and his desire.

> Capitalism has its limits in the specific conditions of production and capitalist circulation, i.e., in capital itself. But capital only functions by reproducing and enlarging these

The Production of Desire

> limits to an always larger scale and in this sense has no limits. It is properly the power of capitalism that its axiomatic (equivalent exchange) is never saturated. . . . the absence of exterior limits is "filled" by expanding interior limits. . . . the axiomatic has no need to write in flesh itself, to mark bodies and organs or to fabricate a memory for men. Contrary to codes the capitalist axiomatic finds in each of its aspects its own organs of execution, perception and memorization. . . . The person has really become "private" to the point that the person is derived from abstract quantities or only becomes concrete as these quantities themselves become concrete. Thus in capital it is the quantities themselves that are marked not the persons.[18]

In breaking down the barriers between human labor, sexuality, and symbolic meaning, capitalism releases subjectivity. Productivity in general, whether it results in objects, meanings, or desires, is the point of the commodity-form. All the external limits to society are internalized; that is, the boundaries to activity no longer confront the subject as objective or externally imposed constraints. The form of control is not the rigid opposition of culture and nature characteristic of the primitive code but a dynamic, in Deleuze and Guattari's language, of deterritorialization and reterritorialization. This double movement is what mistakenly appears to some Marxists as the breakdown of the economy in capitalism.

> On the one hand capitalism can only proceed in endlessly developing the subjective essence of abstract wealth, producing for the sake of producing. But on the other hand, and simultaneously, capitalism can only do this within its own ends, as a determined mode of production. . . . Under the first aspect capitalism never ceases to overcome its own limits, in ever increasing deterritorializations (liberation of productivity and subjectivity) . . . but under the second aspect, strictly complementary, capitalism never stops erecting barriers and limits which are interior, immanent. . . . This is why the limits of capitalism (the falling rate of profit) are never finally realized, rather continually overcome and reproduced. The direct manifestation of this is the simultaneity of the two moments of deterritorialization and reterritorialization.[19]

If there is no economic collapse, where is the weak link in this whole reproduction? Capitalism produces its subjectivity in a personal experience of the social breakdown of boundaries and codes that constrain human productivity and subjectivity. Thus capitalist subjectivity is the experience of a vast indifference and equivalence of objects and identities. Such fragmentation and disintegration of human consciousness appears in Marx's theory as the concept of alienation. In what Marx calls the self-stupefaction of the laborer he paints a picture similar to what Deleuze and Guattari call schizophrenia.

> The need for money is therefore the true need produced by the economic system. . . . Just as it reduces everything to its abstract form, so it reduces itself in the course of its own movement to *quantitative* being. *Excess* and *intemperance* come to be its true norm.
>
> Subjectively, this appears partly in the fact that the extension of products and needs becomes a contriving and ever-calculating subservience to inhuman, sophisticated, unnatural and *imaginary* appetites. Private property does not know how to change crude human need into *human* need. Its idealism is *fantasy, caprice* and *whim*; and no eunuch flatters his despot more basely or uses more despicable means to stimulate his dulled capacity for pleasure in order to sneak a favour for himself than does the industrial eunuch—the producer—in order to sneak for himself a few pieces of silver. . . . He puts himself at the service of the other's most depraved fancies, plays the pimp between him and his needs, excites in him morbid appetites, lies in wait for each of his weaknesses all so that he can then demand the cash for this service of love.[20]

Such artificially produced dependence, for Marx, results in the continuing and necessary degradation and regression of the laborer. "His senses no longer exist," and he becomes, in Marx's words, "a cave dweller" again. But in *L'Anti-Oedipe* there is a side to this human collapse which resists, not through degradation and exhaustion, but in a positive assertion of desire against its rule by the social formation.

According to Deleuze and Guattari, capitalism discovers desire as productivity at the same moment that it grasps culture as the outcome of labor. But this productivity, both as labor and desire, only appears as a personal, private nature. In this manner the initial liberation of productivity that marks the birth of capitalism is continually channeled into the equivalence-form and into commoditization. At the level of desire such integration is expressed in the familial form of exchange known as the Oedipus complex. Desire is thereby domesticated. "Not a word is said about the enormous social, political and historical content of delirium, as if the libido has nothing to do with such things. The only sexual arguments are those which join together sexuality and the familial complex and mythological arguments which consist in making the productive power of the unconscious merely the edifying forces of myth and religion . . . [substituting] simple expressive relations and representative forms for the productive formation of the unconscious. The fundamental question which is ignored and repressed is: Why return to myth? Why take Myth as a model?"[21] The positive side of schizophrenia is that it resists the enforcement of the Oedipus complex and the reduction of desire to the family scene. It is the product of capital that will not enter back into exchange and cannot be channeled back into those social institutions. "The theoretical opposition is not between two classes because the very concept of class as the negation of codes, constitutes only one class (the bourgoisie). . . . the theoretical opposition is elsewhere. . . . It is between the servants of the machine and those who crack up the machinery. Between the regime of the social machines and desiring machines. Between the relatively internal limits and the absolutely external limit . . . between capitalists and schizos."[22]

Deleuze and Guattari put themselves on the side of "a theory and practice which seeks the highest level of schizophrenia." Rather than resist the process that they call deterritorialization we should push it further at all levels. Thus, like Baudrillard, they are critical of all attempts to retain a viewpoint of some stable true needs or permanent use values. However, this confidence in what they call "the revolutionary power of the decoded flux" speaks to an immediacy in their theory and practice which touches on some of the main problems of an otherwise powerful study of Marx and psychoanalysis.

In *L'Anti-Oedipe* the belief in the spontaneity of desire goes hand in hand with the tendency toward a monistic treatment of production. Therefore the spontaneity of desire is an unreflective confidence in the liberating power and resistance to integration of desire released from such territorializations as the Oedipus complex.

The whole analysis of *L'Anti-Oedipe* revolves around the theme that a control over the subject's needs and desires is formed through commodity exchange itself. This kind of approach can already be found in Marx's early *Economic and Philosophic Manuscripts*. "As a man you have, of course, a human relation to my product: you have a *need* of my product. Hence it exists for you as an object of your desire and your will. But your need, your desire, your will, are powerless as regards my product. That means, therefore, that your human nature, which accordingly is bound to stand in intimate relation to my human production, is not your *power* over this production. . . . Your need, your desire, etc., constitute rather the *tie* which makes you dependent on my product. Far from being the means which give you power over my production, they are instead the means for giving me power over you."[23]

Like labor power, desire is domesticated by being introduced into a massive equalization process where it only manifests itself in the identity of the commodity-form. Baudrillard argues similarly when he says that the object/form prefigures need. However, while Deleuze and Guattari do not assume a reference to any "true needs," they do create an ontology which collapses desire into production.

Deleuze and Gauttari's position is adopted as part of their attack on the representational model of desire found in psychoanalysis and is an effort, as we have seen, not to accept the dualistic view of society as divided between production and culture. However, when their argument is extended into the social history of desire, it uncritically assumes that the Oedipus complex marks a decisive and final confrontation with control over desire and that consequently desire will immediately be revolutionary when released from the family structure.

The essence of capitalism for Deleuze and Guattari is that it intensifies desire by liberating productivity. But this subjectivity released through the intensification of production never escapes the limits of abstraction and privatization. Thus it is continually reintegrated into exchange relations and the commodity-form. Abstraction and privatization are the two principal moments of such social decoding in which sexuality, labor, money, and language enter into equivalence. What Deleuze and Guattari have shown is that when labor is transformed in just this way, which is a precondition of capitalism as a social structure, the whole of culture, needs, and desires correspondingly enter into equivalent exchange. This is the materialist basis for a study of culture as production rather than representation or expression. What is unique about capitalism is that the purely negative control exercised by societies which contain and localize desire is replaced by a massive penetration and reduction of the social body to the form of the com-

The Production of Desire

modity. Marx's statement that what is produced is not only the commodity but the need to be satisfied, not only the object but the subject who desires it, conveys just this power of social integration between the culture and the economy.

It is clear from all of Marx's writings that the only way out of this dominance of exchange is in control over labor. The laboring act must be emancipated before humanity can be liberated from that "pimp," as Marx refers to monetary exchange, between production and need. But we are now aware that an objectivistic interpretation of Marx's account of either labor or need leads directly to the concept of base and superstructure. Since culture is then assumed to be the passive reflection of changes at the technical or purely economic level there will be, as Baudrillard shows, an exploitation through control over signs (that is, control over culture) which will form needs and desire independently of the form of labor.

The position of *L'Anti-Oedipe* is more immanent to Marx's thought since it argues that the self-liberation of labor must entail viewing culture as another aspect of production. But in this specific sense of production there is no implication of a reflection relationship between culture and the economy since the concept of production cuts across this distinction. Deleuze and Guattari argue, however, that the weak point of capitalism is no longer what Marx called the "emiseration of the proletariat." Marx argued that increased demands for productivity bring about an increase in surplus value; therefore the rate of profit would depress wages and cause the laboring class to regress. For Deleuze and Guattari the problem now is precisely the productivity of capitalist society at all levels. Capitalism faces not a crisis of impoverishment but a crisis in its ability to continually rechannel productivity into the confines of the commodity-form while expanding the production of value. The crisis of production is not objective; it is in the form of subjectivity produced.

The position of *L'Anti-Oedipe* is that "It is at the level of flux, and not the level of ideology, that the integration of desire is brought about." In other words, desires or needs in a society are not in the sphere of an ideology representing the more concrete activity of labor. By saying desire is a flux, the authors mean that rather than being a simulacrum of production, desire *is* production. We have already considered Baudrillard's argument that need and desire are not natural but are created by society. It would seem that such a position is compatible with the Marxist view that each culture, each superstructure, forms the human subject to correspond to the demands of the mode of production. Such is the basis of Marx's claim that there is no human nature, since man is a historical being. But Deleuze and Guattari are concerned with another issue. How does a society form or create needs and desires that correspond to its economy? The incorrect answer, they argue, is to imagine that needs or desire "stand for," represent, or mirror the production process. On the contrary, a society produces desire much as it produces food, clothing, and shelter. The cultural integration in society does not occur at a separate sphere or sector in the society but occurs simultaneously in the act of production or labor.

One can see a strong connection between Baudrillard's position and that of *L'Anti-Oedipe*. The Marxist notion of superstructure and ideology are at question, but Deleuze and Guattari do not follow Baudrillard in his theory of symbolic exchange. One of the themes in *L'Anti-Oedipe* is that modern social theory has abandoned, to its detriment, the viewpoint of production for that of exchange. But Deleuze and Guattari want to salvage the concept of labor by emancipating it from utilitarian interpretations.

If exchange tries to understand culture at the level of the circulation of goods, persons, or positions, "*L'Anti-Oedipe*, in agreeement with Marx, wants to subordinate such exchange processes to the praxis that sustains and rules the order of exchange.

5. Ideology and Knowledge in Marx

THE orientation of this study has been, both in the discussion of Marx and in the selection of other texts, toward Marxism as a philosophy of action in which culture is defined through the objectification of labor. Such a concept of culture represents a watershed in the history of ideas, primarily because it attacks the traditional theory of cultural autonomy. By emphasizing the way in which culture reflects and even sustains the labor process, Marx had done more than redirect attention to economic factors. He had changed the dominant concept of how human activity formed its world and how human consciousness was in turn formed by that world. The philosopher T. W. Adorno has stated, without even mentioning Marx, the impact of such a fundamental shift in the history of ideas.

> But the greatest fetish of cultural criticism is the notion of culture as such. For no authentic work of art and no true philosophy, according to their very meaning, has ever exhausted itself in itself alone, in its being-in-itself. They have always stood in relation to the actual life-process of society from which they distinguish themselves. Their very rejection of the guilt of life which blindly and callously reproduces itself, their insistence on independence and autonomy, on separation from the prevailing realm of purposes, implies, at least as an unconscious element, the promise of a condition in which freedom is realized. This remains an equivocal promise of culture as long as its existence depends on a bewitched reality and, ultimately, on control over the work of others.[1]

What Marx brought to an end, therefore, was the idea of culture as a separate and autonomous sphere—what Adorno calls its being-in-itself. Culture can no longer claim to distinguish itself from the society and its "life-processes," but the question then arises of the value or meaning of culture. As Marx asked, why do we still find Greek art so moving and aesthetically pleasing? For Adorno the answer is that all culture promises human freedom or expresses that promise implicitly in its forms and modes of expression. For Adorno that promise remains suspended as long as two conditions continue: "bewitchment," which is what Marx called "ideology," and the control over labor. Adorno seems to say that the relation of superstructure and base, in which the culture merely conforms to the demands of the economic infrastructure, is not a universal condition. It is necessitated only as long as there is a need for ideology and control. If the life-processes of the society were themselves freed from the need for control over labor and ideological mystification, then culture would in fact achieve the autonomy it has always falsely claimed for itself.

Adorno's emphasis on the moment of idealism in Marx's concept of culture can be contrasted in turn with the more political emphasis that Antonio Gramsci placed on Marx's approach.

> Every resolution has been preceded by an intense labor of criticism, by the diffusion of culture and the spread of ideas among the masses of men who are at first resistant and think only of solving their own immediate economic and political problems for themselves, who have no ties of solidarity with others. . . . It was through a critique of capitalist civilization that the unified consciousness of the proletariat was or still is being formed, and a critique implies culture, not simply a spontaneous and naturalistic evolution. A critique implies precisely the self-consciousness that Novalis considered to be the end of culture.[2]

A. Gramsci emphasized the moment of critique in Marx. Culture is the way a society expresses itself or states its values and purposes. Criticism is an investigation of society starting from the society's self-presentation and breaking that self-image down by comparing it with the social reality and the repressed realm of labor. In this way cultural criticism leads directly to the arena of political action. Culture is politics in another sphere, since it is the manner in which the members of the society, including those who are being oppressed, becoming self-conscious and therefore critical of their own conditions of life.

One might say that the question animating my inquiry has been which of these "readings" of Marx is correct. Is Marx, as Adorno claims, the true philosopher of culture, realizing the dreams of idealism through the realism of economic analysis? Or, as Gramsci suggests, does Marx become a critic not in the name of philosophy but to turn the philosophy of culture into the politics of culture?

The easiest answer would be that of course both moments are present. No other philosopher was ever more insistent on the unity between the theoretical and the practical than Marx. Certainly one would expect that the two sides of interpretation as represented by Adorno and Gramsci would be present in much of Marx's thought. In fact questions of interpretation in Marx are always simultaneously political and theoretical. The discovery of new texts in Marx's œuvre or the introduction of a new reading or emphasis in how we read Marx changes the very substance of Marxism. In the case of Marx there is no separation from what Marx is supposed to have initiated and our assessment of how his thought should be interpreted. To believe that Marx initiated a science of history is to read him in a certain manner and with a certain emphasis. Since the concept of a science of history is so problematic, it cannot remain as a constant independent of the question of interpretation.

It is for this reason that most commentators have emphasized Marx's use of the term *ideology* when discussing his philosophy of culture. We have already seen that the corresponding term *superstructure* is complex because it establishes a separation between culture and the economy while at the same time claiming that a "determinate" relationship exists between these phenomena. In the case of ideology its appeal is in its contrast with science. Ideology implies that certain ideas are wrong or false because they can be contrasted with knowledge that correctly represents reality. Such a polemical use of the term ideology was continued in the Marxist tradition and finally used to apply to any cultural, philosophical, or literary domain that would automatically be reduced to the rationalization of bourgeois society.

However, Marx's theory of ideology is more complicated than is usually assumed by commentators. The theory of ideology that has been canonized within Marxism is that which is found in *German Ideology*. Using the phrase "camera obscura," Marx treated ideology as a distorted, upside-down vision of the world in which the reality of society, its mode of production, is veiled in the realm of ideas. Ideology represents reality by inverting the relation between ideas and the materialist conditions of history. The purpose of ideology is as a compensation for an impoverished reality (religion) or a defense of the existing society through its rationalization, as in the division between intellectual and manual labor (philosophy). An ideology is perpetuated by a ruling class and is therefore over and above the basic class relations as their justification in ideas.

The Communist Manifesto argues that "the ruling ideas are the ideas of the ruling class." In this way Marx suggests what Gramsci called the "hegemonic" function of ideology as culture. But the context of Marx's political analysis of ideology makes the model of *German Ideology* ambiguous. The point of Marx's statement from *The Communist Manifesto* is that ideology is not merely the possession of the ruling class but that it is internalized by the oppressed classes. The ruling ideas of the society make the claims of class ideology a universal sentiment and opinion of the society or make the claims appear to be completely natural and immutable. If it is clear that the interests of the ruling class are served by a specific ideology, then the question is how that same ideology can become dominant for the entire society?

In his later writings Marx explores this theme in more depth, and most commentators have ignored the fact that Marx modifies, in important ways, the original picture of ideology as found in *German Ideology*. Marx's writings turned, late in his life, almost exclusively to economic theory. Instead of talking about ideology Marx rephrased the question of the effects of exchange on the laborer or the effect of commoditization on the process of production as a whole. The famous "fetishism of commodities" section in *Capital* treats a phenomenon which is not added on above the materialist base but happens internally to the social structure. The culture and its false consciousness are not separate from production but immanent to the activity of production long before they are manifested as ideas of philosophy or religion.

Marx's argument in *Capital* is that the practice of exchange develops a form within the infrastructure. Objects produced by the society are first and foremost formed by the process of production. The commodity form, by creating an abstract equivalence between objects immanent to the production process, creates a relation to the product and its "thing-like objectivity" that also characterizes the society's understanding of its social relations.

It is not surprising that in that section of *Capital* Marx avoids the word ideology and reverts to the older term "fetishism." Commoditization is not a particular class interest, though it is part of a class structure; rather it is a practice belonging exclusively to neither infrastructure nor superstructure. For this reason the form of social relations is internalized throughout the social structure and not just in the ruling class. In the model of *German Ideology* it appeared that form and meaning were exclusively in the realm of culture and reflected the economic base. Later in Marx the rigid distinction between economy and culture is replaced by a more complex model in which, immanent to production, the form that is also found in culture is in operation. In this way Marx used the concept of labor as a term neither exclusively in the economy nor opposed to culture. For Marx culture itself was a kind of praxis.

The interpretations or criticisms of Marx I have discussed are all related to the concept of labor. In the case of Deleuze and Guattari there is an attempt to draw out the implications of a philosophical reading of labor or production. In their work production takes on a meaning which is not exhausted by the technical activity of labor and can encompass the whole sphere of need and desire. Baudrillard's argument is that concentration on labor in Marx is at the cost of understanding the sphere of consumption and what Goux called the symbolic. Baudrillard's point is that Marxism as a system is built on a reduction of human experience to the narrow confines of the laboring process.

I began by emphasizing the philosophical roots and implications of Marx's use of the concept of labor. In this way I suggested that one's reading of Marx as an economic determinist could be set aside, and a more complex and richer philosopher of society would emerge. It is now time to consider not whether Marx interpreted culture as part of the process of objectification (that is, as part of his concept of labor) but whether that interpretation still leaves out of the social process such aspects of culture as need, consumption, or symbolism.

Though Baudrillard's criticisms of Marx are extremely penetrating on the problem of use value, his overall philosophical view of Marx is predated by the work of Hannah Arendt and Jurgen Habermas. In her most important work, *The Human Condition*, Arendt presents Marx as the key figure in a dialogue with traditional philosophy over the status of human action. Marx's definition of man as essentially a laboring being should be seen, Arendt argues, as a polemical thesis directed against a continuous theme in the history of philosophy, that of man as a rational animal. The change from Aristotle's rational animal to the *animal laborans* is, in Arendt's view, a concise way of questioning the basic philosophical presuppositions that reinforce the ideal of contemplation over activity and degrade the material world in relation to a world of intellectual essences.

Here we have one of the key themes in Marx's critical reevaluation of culture. Marx had argued that philosophy repressed reference to material life, especially the labor of humanity, in the name of viewing reality as fundamentally a spiritual process. Such a view finds its parallel in the deification of culture as a higher realm and a privilege of the contemplative life. Marx, of course, was not the first to suggest that philosophy's defense of the privilege of contemplation is based on class. Aristotle had indeed recognized the link between philosophy and the aristocracy and had defended the institution of slavery on its ultimate service to the man of wisdom. What Marx had suggested was both a theory of the connection among ideas, culture, and labor in his theory of ideology and a project for discovering certain correlations or constant relationships between intellectual and manual labor based on a study of the economy and its social relations.

Arendt considers it fundamental to her effort to resurrect the neo-Aristotelian problem of philosophy and public life. Therefore her book is almost entirely a reply to Marx. Though Arendt takes the issue as a philosophical one, she interprets Marx as a thinker who stressed only the polemical and destructive aspects of criticism. Marx did not have a completed philosophy; his is fragmented and inconsistent, and Arendt is correct in arguing that Marx resisted developing a complete philosophical system. There is every reason to believe that Marx, from the very beginning, rejected the traditional philosophical enterprise of speculative systems. The question of inconsistency depends, however, on the cogency of Arendt's reading of Marx.

The conception of man as a laboring being is a weakness of Marxism, Arendt argues, because such a concept deepens the central crisis of the modern world. Human activity is seen as only what is practical or necessitated by nature. Modern theories that are supposed to be in opposition to Marxism, such as behaviorism and utilitarianism, are instead, in Arendt's view, similar because they deny value to the human activities of speech, discourse, and reason. For Arendt, it is the power of speech, rather than labor, that distinguishes man from the natural world and provides the foundation for community and social life. Therefore she views Marx's theory of labor as purely functional and utilitarian. Arendt views Marx as a continuator rather than a critic of the viewpoints of political economy. Marx's error, to put her argument succinctly, is that he confuses the instrumental activity of work with the human action of communication and therefore provides no place in theory (or, consequently, in society) for human interaction beyond the realm of necessity. Culture for Arendt begins where the instrumental interaction with nature ends. Culture is possible for humanity not because man is an *animal laborans* but because he speaks.

A consequence of this confusion in Marx between labor and action is, Arendt argues, the theory of ideology and superstructure. In her view Marx treats all culture as a rationalization for the utilization of labor. Therefore all culture is contained in the concept of ideology or the superstructure as the section of society justifying existing social relations. By identifying all culture with ideology Marx denies to human beings any honest or real interaction in their speech and discourse. All human communication is, for Marx, hypocrisy, since it is determined by a false consciousness that perpetuates the status quo. But such a position, Arendt continues, reduces all human interaction to brute force. In other words, in conformity with Marx's confusion between labor and action, the theory of ideology turns all human relationships into instrumental projects. Human beings are not to be convinced or persuaded by reason but manipulated by violence.

> The Marxian identification of action with violence implies another fundamental challenge to the tradition which may be more difficult to perceive, but of which Marx, who knew Aristotle very well, must have been aware. The twofold Aristotelian definition of man . . . as a . . . being attaining his highest possibility in the faculty of speech and the life in a polis . . . was that Greeks, living together in a polis, conducted their affairs by means of speech, through persuasion . . . and not by means of violence, through mute coercion. . . . Labor was to the Greeks essentially a nonpolitical, private affair, but violence was related to and established a contact, albeit negative, with other men. Marx's glorification of violence therefore contains the more specific denial of speech, the diametrically opposite and traditionally most human form of intercourse. Marx's theory of ideological superstructures ultimately rests on the anti-traditional hostility to speech and the concomitant glorification of violence.[3]

Not only does Marx's theory of human essence confuse labor with human action but in reducing all human relationships to the instrumental rationality of labor (relationships of means to ends), it eliminates the sphere of communication.

Arendt argues that Marx's failure to distinguish between work and action leads him to a persistent inconsistency. Marx unconsciously realized the limitations of his model, and when faced with actually describing a future society he abandoned labor as the essential character of human life. In fact it would seem that precisely what Marx promises is a society freed from labor and a humanity liberated from that activity which he had formerly called its true essence.

Arendt seems to have specifically in mind a famous comment Marx makes concerning the transition from the "realm of necessity" to the "realm of freedom."

> The realm of freedom actually begins only where labor which is determined by necessity and mundane consideration ceases; thus in the very nature of things it lies beyond the sphere of actual material production. Just as the savage must wrestle with Nature to satisfy his wants . . . so must civilized man, and he must do so in all social formations and under all possible modes of production. . . . [even] achieving this with the least expenditure of energy and under conditions most favourable to, and worthy of, human nature . . . nonetheless still remains a realm of necessity. Beyond it begins that development of human energy which is an end in itself, the true realm of freedom, which, however, can blossom forth only with this realm of necessity as its basis.[4]

Marx's argument is relatively complicated here. First he argues that no matter how advanced the society or favorable the conditions of production, labor is still ruled by the dictate of necessity. Arendt agrees with this point and in fact stresses that precisely because labor is a necessitated and determined action, it is not the form of human activity which defines and distinguishes humanity from nature. After adding that labor remains in all modes of production, Marx then suggests that "beyond" this realm of necessity there is a realm in which "energy . . . is an end in itself." Such a Kantian formulation seems to imply that Marx is here making a distinction between the labor forced by mundane circumstances and labor—or energy—freed from all utility and need. It would seem that true creative freedom is the expenditure of human energy as an end in itself and not as a means to another end. We can pick up the themes of our different commentators on Marx. Marx's use of labor and energy as equivalent and the description of this as an "expenditure" suggests the attitude of Deleuze and Guattari concerning the unity between production and desire. But at the same time, in his reference to the "savage" wrestling with Nature, Marx seems to be committing the error that Baudrillard exposes as an "anthropologism of needs." Marx contrasts the liberated society with a quasi-naturalistic account of need and satisfaction in which the symbolic element is missing and in which the free expenditure of labor is postponed.

What Arendt finds perplexing about this passage in Marx is that it promises a future society without labor, more specifically, a future without labor ruled by necessity. Marx makes the goal of emancipation some kind of leisure society. But if that is the reality of a classless society, Arendt points out, then human beings would find themselves bereft of what makes them essentially human—the activity of labor. If the critique of capitalism rests on what Marx calls the alienation of labor, then on Marx's own terms such alienation would be reexperienced in a society without classes.

> Marx's attitude toward labor and thus toward the very center of his thought has never ceased to be equivocal. While it was an "eternal necessity imposed by nature" and the most human and productive of man's activities, the revolution, according to Marx, has not the task of emancipating the laboring classes but of emancipating man from labor; only when labor is abolished can the "realm of freedom" supplant the "realm of necessity". . . . In all stages of his work Marx defines man as an *animal laborans* and then leads him into a society in which the greatest and most human power is no longer necessary.[5]

Arendt thought that Marx only believed that man could be liberated in this way because he confused action with labor. Marx was fundamentally utilitarian and instrumental in his view of human life; therefore he tried to describe liberation as a mechanical model of the expenditure of energy. "The hope that inspired Marx . . . that free time eventually will emancipate men from necessity and make the *animal laborans* productive—rests on the illusion of a mechanistic philosophy which assumes that labor power, *like any other energy,* can never be *lost*, so that if it is not spent and exhausted in the drudgery of life it will automatically nourish other 'higher' activities."[6]

Arendt's central theme is that all modern philosophy has been seduced by the pragmatism and utilitarianism of the modern age to the detriment of activity that is an "end in itself." Though Marx mentions such action he still hopes to produce it from labor dictated by necessity. But Arendt's argument seems to oversimplify vastly the way in which Marx defends the centrality of labor. Marx does not begin with labor as drudgery or as a natural necessity but rather as a specific form of social activity. Rather than eternalizing the relationship of labor to the world, Marx sought to historicize it and understand the differences and mutability of the relationship. From the historical character of labor Marx does derive an ontology. In that ontology he states that objectification is part of the human condition. Humanity stands in relation to a world of objects that it itself forms and toward which it acts. Such standing against objects (*Gegenstandlichkeit*) is Marx's basis for every other human relationship and activity.

By stating an ontology of society, Marx does not, as Arendt suggests, assume a causal relationship between objectification and the specific historical form of labor. The activity of objectification is what makes it possible for there to be a causal and determined aspect to man's social nature. Rather than appealing to some automatic change Marx seems, on the contrary, to emphasize that it is only under the blind necessity of nature or alienation that change appears automatic, determined, or inevitable. Though Marx was wary of thinkers who downplayed the serious side of labor, he viewed labor as a self-realization process, not a causal network of instrumentalism. "Labour attains its measure . . . through the aim to be attained and the obstacle to be overcome in attaining it. . . . this overcoming of obstacles is itself a liberating activity . . . self-realization, objectification of the subject, and hence real freedom . . . attractive work, the individual's self-realization is by no means mere fun, mere amusement. . . . Really free working, e.g., composing, is at the same time precisely the most damned seriousness, the most intense exertion."[7]

To bring to a summary my comments on Marx's use of labor let us briefly look at another criticism of Marx found in the work of Jurgen Habermas. In the vein of Arendt's approach to society, Habermas divides society into two spheres, one of communication or human interaction and one of technical and instrumental control. Interaction and communication are essentially the means by which a society forms a concept of itself or creates its social identity. It includes not only what Arendt calls speech and discourse but, more specifically, forms of social consciousness, morality, and the organization of political participation. Therefore interaction is concerned with questions of value, meaning, and justification. In contrast the sphere of technical and instrumental control is concerned with utility and power since its purpose is to successfully use the natural world for the satisfaction of needs. Appropriately its logic is one of means and ends and its action practical. A society will always encompass both these spheres, and Habermas compares his approach to Marx's distinction between relations of production and forces of production.

Habermas discusses Marx in terms of a distinction between production and the symbolic. The symbolic is fundamentally the sphere of interaction of consciousness, and therefore it would encompass what Marx called the superstructure. Habermas argues that Marx pursued a reductionist account because he tried to explain symbolic structures by turning to the production process. But the production process is essentially instrumental, and therefore Marx ends up reducing symbolism to natural necessity. When Marx dealt with wholly symbolic activities such as philosophy or art, in Habermas' view he tried to picture them as identical to the act of labor. Marx thought that philosophy and art, for example, should become more like the material transformation of the world that is found in labor. But this, Habermas concludes, naturalizes symbolism and treats culture as an extension of utility.

> Marx does not actually explicate the interrelationship of interaction and labor, but instead, under the unspecific title of social praxis, reduces the one to the other, namely, communicative acts to instrumental acts. . . . for Marx instrumental action, the productive activity which regulates the material interchange of the human species with the natural environment, becomes the paradigm for the generation of all the categories; everything is resolved into the self-motion of production.

> If Marx had not thrown together interaction and work under the label of social praxis (Praxis) and had instead related the materialist conception of synthesis likewise to the accomplishments of instrumental action and the nexuses of

communicative action, then the idea of a science of man would not have been obscured by the identification with natural science.[8]

Though Habermas, unlike Arendt, grants that Marx may have tried to develop a philosophical concept of labor, he still agrees that the concept of objectification cannot apply to both symbolic activities, such as morality and aesthetics, and to the material satisfaction of needs through instrumental control over nature. But it seems to me that Habermas' very distinction is problematic. For example, if we say that instrumental action is designed to satisfy needs, we will be forced to realize, at some point in the analysis, that a need and its satisfaction are just as symbolic, cultural, and historical as religion, morality, or art. To understand a need it is necessary to understand the whole society and its historical mediation. Nature per se gives us no guidance to utility or instrumentality. The point is not that symbolic structure must be separate from instrumental action but that instrumental action is a symbolic, not a natural, category. When Marx defined a mode of production as a mode of life, he meant to show that a society is a totality. Therefore technical control is just as cultural, symbolic, and socially mediated as the realm of communication. To put the same point another way, communication is just as much an act of self-objectification or purposive action, in Marx's language, as the labor process.

My argument concerning Habermas is that production is already symbolic. The relationship to need or utility is not distinct from all the other cultural forms in the society. The communicative system and the instrumental system are not distinct spheres, each having a separate logic of action. Therefore there is a point to Marx's attempt to find a single form of activity at the base of different strategies or logics. As Marshall Sahlins argues, "All utilities are symbolic. In so far as 'utility' is a concept of 'need' appropriate to a certain cultural order, it must include a representation, by the way of concrete properties of the object, of the differential relation between persons. . . . The system of needs must always be relative, not accountable as such by physical necessity, hence symbolic by definition."[9]

I also agree with both Baudrillard and Sahlins that if Marx is interpreted to retain a utilitarian or naturalistic concept of labor, then Marxism continues the same epistemological assumptions as bourgeois political economy. The distinction between base and superstructure will then be eternalized as a natural condition of all societies, and the role of the economy will reduce to a simplistic determinism.

Utility and need are not the reference of production but cultural restraints or forms imposed on human activity. Marx in his analysis of commoditization did show how objects are naturalized or seen as autonomous from social production. The "thinglike" character of the world of commodities hides their social character and makes it appear that these specific historical relations of production are immutable and natural. According to Baudrillard, Marx's failure was that he did not extend his critique of fetishism to the category of use value. Marx assumed that the relationship to need falls outside of a social analysis and is therefore independent of any particular society. As Baudrillard concluded: "Marx shattered the myth of *Homo economicus*, the myth which sums up the whole process of the naturalization of the system of exchange values, the market and surplus value and its forms. But he did so in the name of labor power's emergence in action, of man's own power to give rise to the value of his labor. Isn't this a similar fiction, a similar naturalization—another wholly arbitrary convention, a simulation model bound to *code* all human material and every contingency of desire and exchange in terms of value, finality and production."[10]

Baudrillard concludes, as does Arendt, that the viewpoint of man as a laboring being is reductionist and capitulates to the very values of industrial society that Marx claims to oppose. We can note in passing that both Arendt and Baudrillard appeal to something like Marx's notion of ideology since they imply that Marx, like the political economists, is "unconsciously" internalizing and promoting the values of the dominant social forces. But it seems to me that the main question is whether labor, utility, and biological determinism are necessarily connected in Marx's theory. I have already argued that Marx does not equate his concept of labor with the labor theory of value in political economy. Therefore while interpretations emphasizing naturalistic and utilitarian elements in Marx are possible, it is also quite possible to shift the emphasis as I have done here in chapter 1. The main question then is why choose that aspect rather than others in presenting Marx.

I have suggested that certain aspects of Marx are more philosophically stimulating than others. But let us now assume that our critics have accepted a more developed concept of labor. We can still return to the main criticisms. Does Marx eliminate in his theory the whole sphere of life outside of the production process (that is, the sphere of culture)? Should we seek to explain society as Marx does through a single human activity or model of action?

To answer the first objection I tried to show how the Hegelian theory of objectification, which is a part of Marx's concept of labor, could serve as a general theory of cultural activity and in fact precedes the distinction between culture and economy. We have seen that in a general fashion Marx's theory can deal with such wide-ranging social experiences as sexuality and literature without adopting a reductionistic approach. Habermas, however, clearly argues that it is wrong on principle to attempt to find a single form of activity or model of action in the social sciences because of the inherent dual nature of social structure as divided between instrumental action and interaction. I feel that Habermas' more eclectic approach weakens rather than strengthens social theory. Even if we were to accept his a priori distinction between communication and instrumental action, his approach, like Goux's, places total emphasis on the ability of a theory simply to incorporate social phenomena under different categories. Such a categorical organization of theory produces only the illusion of an explanation since it builds in qualifications that protect the theory against difficult examples. Marx's theory has the merit of being more critical and therefore more extreme in its claim. We learn more by working within the narrower limits of Marx's hypothesis about labor than we would in more easily accommodating the data to Habermas' more flexible and qualified hypothesis about interaction.

In his brilliant study of Marxism and aesthetics, Raymond Williams poses a central issue: "The insertion of economic determinations into cultural studies is of course the special contribution of Marxism, and there are times when its simple insertion is an evident advance. But in the end it can never be a simple insertion, since what is really required, beyond the limiting formulas, is restoration of the whole social material process and specifically of cultural production as social and material."[11]

In answer to how the "whole social material process" of culture can be reconstructed, I have suggested looking to Marx on labor rather than on ideology or superstructure. In my view Marx defended the labor theory of value in *Capital* not because that is how to solve problems in economics but because it made labor a central phenomenon of society; but he knew also that it was wrong. Marx criticized labor as value not because of limitations in economic theory but because labor for Marx was not primarily a form of exchange nor was it reducible to the utility of production for the market. Those issues are properly philosophical, and Marx's disputes with political economy were over respective conceptions of human society. Consequently a whole history of Marxist interpretation has been muddled by the search for a Marxist economics or "economic laws" when those concepts have only a "critical" meaning in Marx.

But there is another reason that steers me away from Marx's use of ideology and superstructure in a conception of culture and its relationship to the infrastructure. In addition to the inherent problematic character of these terms, which I have tried to show, ideology and superstructure are associated with claims that Marx established a science of history or society.

By emphasizing that labor is a philosophical concept in Marx, I have in effect distinguished it from the effort to give scientific explanations. To some this will seem a strange defense of Marx, since it is assumed that the highest compliment paid a theory is to identify it as a science. Without denigrating in the least the immense importance of science in the larger domain of human knowledge, it is simply reductive to reject or deny value to knowledge and reasoning that does not replicate the approach of the sciences. Unfortunately both defenders and opponents of Marx have been trapped inside this highly restrictive prejudice and have tried to focus all discussion of Marx on empirical confirmation or lack of confirmation of his theory.

Labor, unlike the concepts of ideology and superstructure, is not itself an explanation of any social phenomenon. To be generous one could say that Marx outlined the preconditions for making hypothetical explanations of social change. In his work, however, Marx emphasized the critical distinction between his own fundamental presuppositions and those of his most serious rival, political economy. Of course I am aware that Marx did claim for himself a scientific approach to society. But it must be remembered first that the relationship of *Wissenschaft* to philosophy in the tradition that Marx knew cannot be superimposed on our present, more opposed sense of these terms. In addition, I hold that Marx's attitude to his critical treatment of political economy was fundamentally philosophical, or methodological, to use a more neutral term, and that the theory of labor is what makes it possible for there to be any systematic knowledge of society.

My point can be made somewhat more sharply by appealing to some recent philosophy of science.[12] Imre Lakatos, in reacting against what he believed to be a dogmatic version of Popper's falsificationist position on the definition of science, suggested what he called "the methodology of research programmes with a metaphysical core." Karl Popper had held that in view of the logical impossibility of proof through induction, no scientific theory could claim to be true on the basis of confirming evidence. However, if theories were stated in a clear enough manner, they could be tested so as to disprove or falsify them. Unlike confirmation, a theory need only be falsified once to be disproved; therefore Popper suggested that science proceeds by "conjectures" and their consequent refutations through experiment. The difference between science and nonscience became for Popper falsifiability. Nonscientific knowledge was knowledge that was so stated that no one could falsify it. For example, psychoanalysts, according to Popper, produce explanations of human motivation, but these explanations are of such a nature that even if the individual did the opposite of what was expected that would not invalidate the explanation. Popper's approach to Marx, on the other hand, was to say that, unlike psychoanalysis, Marx did produce a falsifiable hypothesis in the fashion of good science. Marx's view of society set out specific consequences which should occur; but since Popper concludes that these changes did not occur, the proletariat were not impoverished, and capitalism was able to introduce structural reform, Marx's hypotheses were falsified.

I am vastly simplifying a complex area of contemporary philosophy when I say that Lakatos and other philosophers of science, specifically Thomas Kuhn and Hilary Putnam, began to criticize this "simplified" version of falsification. The debate was in terms of the natural sciences; essentially it was argued that in science a theory is rejected not by a disconfirming observation but only by another theory. Therefore Lakatos argued that science presents us with certain "research programmes" in which there is a highly philosophical or metaphysical "core" that can be neither proved nor disproved. Such a core is necessary and allows a science to form certain hypotheses. In the face of disconfirming evidence, what the scientist usually does is preserve the theory by making certain "ad hoc" adjustments. Lakatos' position was that the scientist should make such adjustments and not immediately abandon his theory. The only problem is that at a certain point research in a theory may begin to "degenerate" due to numerous ad hoc adjustments of the theory, and then it is no longer a fruitful tool for problem solving.

Let me now extrapolate these comments to the case of Marx. The Lakatosian view would be that Marxists were wholly justified in reacting to the possible disconfirming evidence of structural change in capitalism without revolution by making adjustments in the theory which could explain why the proletariat did not act or why reforms would not ultimately prove effective. My point is not whether this shows that Marxism is a science, since Lakatos agrees with Popper and views Marxism as a "degenerating" research program. My point is that the "metaphysical" core of the research program is basically how I have tried to characterize Marx's use of the concept of labor. If one were to relate Marx's philosophy of culture and society to the social sciences it would be through this core conception of a research program. That explains why Marx concentrated on his philosophical distinction from political economy. While Marx meant by "metaphysical" something quite different than Lakatos, Marx always held philosophical clarification in high esteem. Once this point is ignored, too much attention is paid to the more limited explanatory devices of superstructure and ideology when discussing Marx's fundamental theory.

The issue about the status of Marx's theory as a science of society has always been mired in confusion because of the orthodox claim that Marx was scientific by virtue of his materialism. Certainly if by materialism one means that social phenomena are explainable and rational on their own terms without invoking the will of God, this is trivially true. But the fact is that no science can rest content with the idea of physical or material causes since once the focus shifts in a science the distinction between material and immaterial correspondingly alters. But my point is more basically that Marx represents neither a science nor a specific hypothesis as Popper claims. Rather Marx outlined a metaphysical (philosophical) conception of society and culture based on a theory of action. Marx's philosophical work was to articulate this idea of society and critically to compare it to alternative ideas. But such a critical enterprise cannot predetermine that there will be a science or that scientific reasoning is even necessary. It may be finally that "knowledge" about society and culture, this vague object of the social sciences, is not the object of any real science. In fact I am persuaded that such is the case but that it is not a reason for despair. But that would involve showing that there are indeed "metaphysical" and evaluative stakes in the distinction between science and nonscientific domains of knowledge which have to be made explicit and criticized. That cannot be done here.[13]

Since Marx's work now stands somewhere between a possible social science and an interpretation of culture, it has not ceased to be interesting to those in either camp. All I have tried to do is shed some light on what Marx's philosophical contribution was, and in this way I can appropriate a famous statement concerning Marx's method by Georg

Lukacs. "Let us assume for the sake of argument that recent research had disproved once and for all every one of Marx's individual theses. . . . every serious 'orthodox' Marxist would still be able to accept all such modern findings without reservation and hence dismiss all of Marx's theses *in toto*—without having to renounce his orthodoxy for a single moment. . . . orthodoxy refers exclusively to method."[14]

It has been traditional to attack this passage in a Popperian way as an example of treating Marxism as a theory which cannot be disproved or as the inherent dogmatism of the Marxist scholar. But I suggest a more generous interpretation. If we ignore for the moment the idiosyncratic use of the term *method* in Lukacs, the distinction he is drawing is between specific explanations and the "metaphysical" core of the theory. Marx's conception of society, the way in which Marx approaches the study of society and culture, makes it possible for society to become an object of explanation. A certain philosophical orientation or interpretation sets the stage for abstractions, the distinction of important from unimportant fact, and certain regularities. The fate of each given explanation, Lukacs argues, is distinct from and is survived by the idea which made each attempt possible.

In offering the concept of labor as Marx's contribution to what Lukacs calls "method," I am not claiming that it will found a social science or prove inviolate against criticism. My only point is that discussion about labor is philosophical in Marx, especially when Marx is looked at in relation to contemporary concerns. I have explained it in relation to other organizing concepts in Marx and have tried to show how it stands in relation to other theories of society as seen in Arendt, Levi-Strauss, or Hegel. But points of criticism must also be raised about a philosophy of culture founded on the model of labor as objectification.

My criticisms of Goux are relevant in that context. Goux confuses the framework, model, or metaphysical core in Marx with the explanation of social phenomena. Goux seems to assume that because he can put a social structure into a schematic model he has explained something. In fact all he has done is to show that Marx's core conception encompasses the relevant data, that it is not an economic determinism, and that it may be posssible to form certain hypotheses in the social sciences on the basis of it. But Goux obviously wants to specify in advance what the concrete relation between phenomena will be, and he treats science as a coherent system of concepts. He makes extravagant claims because he confuses philosophical articulation with scientific research, and that is a complementary problem to a scientism which legislates against any knowledge outside of the model of the natural sciences.

I argued initially that labor should be treated as a complex, philosophical concept that preceded the distinction between economy and culture or nature and symbolism. While Deleuze and Guattari show how labor and production include what is usually opposed in activity as need and desire, they also inflate this point into a vast explanatory model. In an error parallel to Goux's, Deleuze and Guattari do not seem to appreciate that a philosophical or metaphysical framework is an abstraction or heuristic device (which must be judged on its own terms) and is not supported by making a vast number of analogies. Their book demonstrates that Marx's work can be used to integrate different approaches in modern social science. Though that is the value of a philosophical framework, it should not be confused with explanation or allow for "metaphor" to replace the social sciences. I would prefer to make the argument in terms of whether the social sciences are in fact what produce knowledge about society, and I believe that is the critical approach Marx took with political economy.

Marx is finally a characteristic modern thinker. He had hoped to destroy the enterprise of traditional philosophy but in no way wanted to deny the significance of the questions asked by philosophy. He offered instead of a system, which is what Marx meant by metaphysics, a symptomology, to use Nietzsche's phrase, of the modern world. But in constructing his "social hieroglyphics" Marx had to represent speculatively what it was to act, know, and live as social beings. The dilemmas he leaves us with in his speculation are worth considering. On the one hand, Marx gave a sobering demonstration, between Hobbes and Freud, of the cost in terms of oppression and repression that have made society possible and that our culture serves in turn to justify and legitimize with its refinements. But, on the other, in the vast work carried on by humanity Marx always saw more of a promise than a curse.

Notes

CHAPTER 1. MARX'S CONCEPT OF LABOR

1. Marx and Engels, *Collected Works*, 4:272.
2. Ibid., p. 276.
3. Ibid., p. 300.
4. Ibid., p. 225.
5. Ibid., pp. 332–33.
6. Giambattista Vico, *The New Science*, p. 52.
7. Hegel, *Philosophy of History*, p. 241.
8. Ibid., pp. 52–53.
9. Marx and Engels, *Collected Works*, 4:333.
10. Marx and Engels, *German Ideology*, p. 460.
11. Marx, *Capital*, 1:283–84.
12. Ibid.
13. Ibid., p. 290.
14. Ibid., p. 167.
15. Marx, *Contribution to Critique of Political Economy*, p. 20.
16. Marx, *Grundrisse*, p. 110.
17. *German Ideology*, p. 32.
18. *Grundrisse*, p. 111.

CHAPTER 2. THE ECONOMIC AND THE SYMBOLIC IN CULTURE

1. "In effect the situation introduces a series of events in which the body and internal organs of the subject constitute a kind of theatre"—Levi-Strauss, *Anthropologie structurale*, p. 123.
2. "The cure will consist of rendering thinkable a situation given first in external terms; and to make the mind accept pains the body refuses to tolerate. It is of no importance that the mythology of the shaman does not correspond to objective reality; the woman giving birth believes it and she is a member of a society that believes it" (ibid., pp. 213–14).
3. Ibid., pp. 214–15.

Notes

4. "The notion of manipulation which is central to the intelligibility of the shamanistic cure must be broadened in its traditional definition. It is neither wholly a manipulation of ideas nor manipulation of organs because the common condition remains that it is done through symbols, i.e., through the significant equivalents of meaning [*signifie*] belonging to another order or reality" (ibid., p. 221).

5. Ibid., p. 218.
6. Ibid., p. 220.
7. Ibid., p. 223.
8. "Introduction à l'œuvre de Marcel Mauss," p. xix.
9. Ibid., p. xvi.
10. Levi-Strauss, *The Elementary Structures of Kinship*, p. 84.
11. *The Savage Mind*, pp. 130, 263.
12. Marx, *Grundrisse*, p. 84.
13. *The Elementary Structures of Kinship*, pp. 8–10.
14. Marx, *Capital*, 1:167.
15. Marx, *A Contribution to the Critique of Political Economy*, pp. 28–29.
16. *Capital*, 1:142.
17. Ibid., p. 181.
18. Ibid., pp. 183–84.
19. "The forms which stamp products as commodities and which are therefore the preliminary requirements for the circulation of commodities, already possess the fixed quality of natural forms of social life before man seeks to give an account, not of their historical character, for in his eyes they are immutable, but of their content and meaning" (ibid., p. 168).
20. Marx, *Grundrisse*, p. 92.
21. J-J. Goux, *Economie et symbolique: Marx, Freud*, p. 19.
22. Ibid., p. 38. One can find similar points made within linguistics itself. "Semen, excreta and words are communicative products. . . . At the far root, their symbolic significance, the rites, taboos and fantasies which they evoke, and certain of the social controls of their use, are inextricably interwoven" (George Steiner, *After Babel*, p. 39).
23. Malinowski, *Argonauts of the Western Pacific*, p. 83.
24. *Capital*, 1:176n.
25. Goux, pp. 222–23: "A mode of writing is representative of a mode of signified exchange. This mode of signification is also manifested in other cultural aspects, such as aesthetic production. There exists a correspondence between the mode of production in general, economic exchange and the mode of signification in particular. . . . it is as if it were possible to discover the same mode of symbolization in all characteristic practices. . . . Law, subjective relations, religion, sexuality, parental relations . . . entail the same dialectic of symbolization."
26. Ibid., p. 229.
27. Ibid., p. 69.
28. Ibid., pp. 126–27.
29. Ibid., p. 76.
30. Ibid., p. 87.

Notes 97

CHAPTER 3. OBJECTS AND UTILITY

1. "But the alternatives offered by Ricardo's pessimism and Marx's revolutionary promise are probably of little importance. Such a system of options represents nothing more than the two possible ways of examining the relation of anthropology and history as they are established by economics through the notion of scarcity and labour. For Ricardo, history fills the void produced by anthropological finitude and expressed in perpetual scarcity, until the moment when a point of definitive stabilization is attained; according to the Marxist interpretation, history, by dispossessing man of his labour, causes the positive form of his finitude to spring into relief—his material truth is finally liberated. . . . But these are merely derived differences which stem first and last from a doxological knowledge. Marxism introduced *no real discontinuity*; . . . Though it is in opposition to the bourgeois theories of economics, and though this opposition leads it to use the project of a radical reversal of history as a weapon against them, that conflict and that project nevertheless have as their condition of possibility, not the reworking of all history, but an event . . . that prescribed . . . both nineteenth century bourgeois economics and nineteenth century revolutionary economics" (M. Foucault, *The Order Of Things: An Archaeology of the Human Sciences*, pp. 261–62).

2. Jean Baudrillard, *The Mirror of Production*, p. 19.

3. Baudrillard, *Pour une critique de l'économie politique du signe*, pp. 174–75.

4. "We call the *form/object* the abstract equivalent of utilities, we also say that the *form/object is only the developed form of the form/commodity*. In other words, the same logic (and the same fetishism) operates on both sides of the commodity, use value and exchange value, as specified by Marx" (ibid., p. 160).

5. Ibid., pp. 176–77.

6. Baudrillard's point could be formulated as the claim that Marx perpetuates an economistic definition of "needs" and "use value." Baudrillard defines consumption "not as traditional political economy defines it (namely, the reinversion of economic exchange into use value, as a moment in the production cycle) but as the conversion of economic exchange value into exchange/sign value" (ibid., p. 129).

7. Ibid., p. 155.

8. Ibid., p. 157.

9. "Wishing itself beyond labor but *in its continuation*, the sphere of play is always merely the aesthetic sublimation of labor's constraints. With this concept we remain rooted in the problematic of necessity and freedom, a typically bourgeois problematic whose double ideological expression has always been the institution of a reality principle (repression and sublimation, the principle of labor) and its formal overcoming in an ideal transcendence" (*Mirror of Production*, p. 40).

10. Ibid., p. 31.

11. "After the Requiem for the Dialectic, it is necessary to sound the Re-

quiem for Infra and Superstructure" (*Pour une critique*, p. 207). See also the argument concerning the difference between Baudrillard's concept of "ambivalence" and the dialectical theory of negation (p. 263 f.).

12. *Capital*, 1:138, *Grundrisse*, p. 168.

13. "Labour . . . is an eternal natural necessity which *mediates* the metabolism between man and nature, and therefore human life itself" (*Capital*, 1:133).

14. *Grundrisse*, p. 92.

15. Foucault, "Preface to Transgression," in *Language, Counter-Memory, Practice*, pp. 49–50.

16. *Pour une critique*, pp. 261–62.

17. Ibid., pp. 266–67.

Chapter 4. The Production of Desire

1. G. Deleuze and F. Guattari, *L'Anti-Oedipe: Capitalisme et schizophrenie*.

2. Ibid., p. 284

3. Marx, *Grundrisse*, p. 104.

4. *L'Anti-Oedipe*, pp. 291–92.

5. Ibid., p. 293.

6. Ibid., pp. 359–60.

7. Ibid., p. 403.

8. Ibid., p. 169.

9. In speaking of the primitive social formation Deleuze and Guattari say that "The unities are never persons in the 'private' sense of the word but in *series* which determine the connection, disjunction and conjuncture of organs. This is why fantasies are group fantasies. It is a collective investment of organs which roots desire in the *socius* and reunites social and desiring production in the earth as totality. Our modern societies, on the contrary, have proceeded in a vast privatisation of organs, which corresponds to the decoding of the flux, to its being made abstract" (ibid., p. 167). Along the same lines of argument is this quote from Marx concerning the emergence of exchange, which I have already discussed in the development of Marx's theory of exchange: "The less the social power of the medium of exchange (and at this stage it is still closely bound to the nature of the direct product of labor and the direct needs of partners in exchange), the greater must be the power of the community which binds the individual" (*Grundrisse*, p. 157).

10. *L'Anti-Oedipe*, pp. 179–80.

11. Ibid., pp. 235–36.

12. "In contradistinction to the old gentile organization, the state, first, divides its subjects *according to territory*. . . . The second is the establishment of a *public* power which no longer directly coincides with the population organizing itself as an armed force. . . . This public power consists not merely of armed people but also of material adjuncts, prisons and institutions of coercion of all kinds" (Engels, *The Origin of the Family, Private Property and the State*, p. 159, my italics). Deleuze and Guattari's section on primitivism and

barbarism is an extended interpretation of this text by Engels. Engels' arguments against Karl Kautsky's economic treatment of primitive society and his value to anthropology are discussed by Levi-Strauss in *Anthropologie structurale*, p. 374 f.

13. Marx, *A Contribution to the Critique of Political Economy*, p. 215.
14. *L'Anti-Oedipe*, p. 164.
15. Ibid., p. 180.
16. Ibid., pp. 266–67.
17. Ibid., pp. 294–95.
18. Ibid., pp. 297–98.
19. Ibid., p. 309.
20. Marx and Engels, *Collected Works*, vol. 3 (1843–44), p. 307.
21. *L'Anti-Oedipe*, p. 67.
22. Ibid., p. 303.
23. Marx and Engels, *Collected Works*, 3:225.

CHAPTER 5. IDEOLOGY AND KNOWLEDGE IN MARX

1. T. Adorno, *Prisms*, p. 23.
2. A. Gramsci, *Selected Political Writings, 1910–1920*, p. 12.
3. H. Arendt, *Between Past and Present*, pp. 22–23.
4. Marx, *Capital*, vol. 3, p. 820.
5. Arendt, *The Human Condition*, p. 611.
6. Ibid., p. 133.
7. Marx, *Grundrisse*, p. 611.
8. J. Habermas, *Theory and Practice*, p. 140; *Knowledge and Human Interests*, p. 42.
9. M. Sahlins, *Culture and Practical Reason*, p. 150.
10. J. Baudrillard, *The Mirror of Production*, p. 19.
11. R. Williams, *Marxism and Literature*, p. 138.
12. My sources for this brief discussion of some themes in philosophy of science are K. Popper, *Conjectures and Refutations*; I. Lakatos and A. Musgrave (eds.), *Criticism and the Growth of Knowledge*; and T. Kuhn, *The Structure of Scientific Revolutions*.
13. A critical discussion of both the social sciences and the distinction between science and ideology has been begun by Michel Foucault in both *Archaeology of Knowledge* and *The Order of Things: An Archaeology of the Human Sciences*.
14. G. Lukacs, *History and Class Consciousness*, p. 1.

Bibliography

Adorno, T. W. *Prisms.* Translated by Samuel and Shierry Weber. London: Spearmen, 1967.
Adorno, T. W., and Horkheimer, M. *Dialectic of Enlightenment.* Translated by Mathew J. O'Connel. New York: Seabury Press, 1973.
Althusser, L., et al. *For Marx.* Translated by Ben Brewster. New York: Vintage, 1970.
──── . *Lenin and Philosophy.* Translated by Ben Brewster. New York: Monthly Review Press, 1971.
──── . *Lire Le Capital.* Vols. 1 and 2. Paris: Gallimard, 1970.
──── . *Politics and History: Montesquieu, Rousseau, Hegel and Marx.* Translated by Ben Brewster. London: New Left Books, 1972.
──── . *Reading Capital.* Translated by Ben Brewster. New York: Pantheon, 1970.
Anderson, P. *Considerations on Western Marxism.* London: New Left Books, 1977.
Arendt, H. *Between Past and Present.* London: Penguin Books, 1977.
──── . *The Human Condition.* Chicago: University of Chicago Press, 1974.
Aron, R. *Marxismes imaginaires: D'une sainte famille à l'autre.* Paris: Gallimard, 1970.
Axelos, K. *Marx, Penseur de la technique.* Paris: Editions de Minuit, 1967.
Badiou, A. "Le (re) commencement du matérialisme dialectique." *Critique* 240 (1967): 439–67.
──── . *Le Concept de modèle.* Paris: Maspero, 1969.
Balibar, E. *Cinq etudes du matérialisme historique.* Paris: Maspero, 1974.
──── . *Reading Capital.* Translated by Ben Brewster. New York: Pantheon, 1970.
Barthes, R. *Mythologies.* Translated by Annette Lavers. New York: Hill and Wang, 1972.
Baudrillard, J. *The Mirror of Production.* Translated by Mark Poster. St. Louis: Telos Press, 1975.
──── . *Pour une critique de l'économie politique du signe.* Paris: Gallimard, 1972.
Bauman, Z. *Culture as Praxis.* London: Routledge and Kegan, 1973.

Bibliography

Benjamin, W. *Illuminations*. Edited and with an introduction by Hannah Arendt. Translated by Harry Zohn. New York: Schocken, 1969.
Brown, N. O. *Life against Death: The Psychoanalytic Meaning of History*. New York: Random House, 1965.
Colletti, L. *From Rousseau to Lenin*. Translated by J. Merrington and J. White. London: New Left Books, 1972.
———. *Marxism and Hegel*. Translated by Lawrence Garner. London: New Left Books, 1973.
Corvez, M. *Les Structuralistes*. Paris: Aubier-Montaigne, 1969.
Deleuze, G., and Guattari, F. *L'Anti-Oedipe: Capitalisme et schizophrenie*. Vol. 1. Paris: Editions du Minuit, 1972.
Derrida, J. *L'Ecriture et la différence*. Paris: Seuil, 1967.
———. *Of Grammatology*. Translated by Gayatra Chakravarty Spivak. New Haven: Yale University Press, 1977.
———. *Positions*. Paris: Editions de Minuit, 1972.
———. *Speech and Phenomena*. Translated by David A. Allison. Evanston: Northwestern University Press, 1973.
Dufrenne, M. *Pour l'homme*. Paris: Seuil, 1968.
Engels, F. *The Origin of the Family, Private Property and the State*. Translated by Robert Vernon. New York: Pathfinder Press, 1972.
Establet, R., et al. *Lire Le Capital*. Vol. 2. Paris: Maspero, 1965.
Fages, J. B. *Le Structuralisme en procès*. Paris: Privat, 1968.
Foucault, M. *The Archaeology of Knowledge*. Translated by A. M. Sheridan Smith. New York: Pantheon, 1972.
———. *Language, Counter-Memory, Practice*. Translated and edited by Donald F. Bouchard. Ithaca: Cornell University Press, 1977.
———. *The Order of Things: An Archaeology of the Human Sciences*. New York: Pantheon, 1970.
Franklin, M. "On Hegel's Theory of Alienation and Its Historic Force." *Tulane Studies in Philosophy* (1960).
Freud, S. *Civilization and Its Discontents*. Translated by James Strachey. New York: Norton Library, 1961.
Gabel, J. *False Consciousness: An Essay on Reification*. Translated by Margaret A. Thompson and Kenneth A. Thompson. New York: Harper and Row, 1975.
Gaché, R. *Die hybride Wissenschaft: Zur Mutation des Wissenschaftsbegriff bei Emile Durkheim und im Strukturalismus von Claude Levi-Strauss*. Stuttgart: Metzlersche und Poeschel Verlag, 1973.
Garaudy, R. *Marxism in the Twentieth Century*. Translated by Rene Hague. New York: Scribner's, 1970.
Gay, P. *Bernstein and the Dilemma of Democratic Socialism*. New York: Columbia University Press, 1952.
Geras, N. "Althusser's Marxism: An Account and Assessment." *New Left Review* 71 (1972): 57–86.
Glucksmann, A. "Un Structuralist ventriloque." *Les Temps Modernes* 250 (1967).
Glucksmann, M. *Structuralist Analysis and Contemporary Social Thought*. London: Routledge and Kegan, 1974.

Bibliography

Godelier, M. *Perspectives in Marxist Anthropology*. Translated by Robert Brain. New York: Cambridge University Press, 1977.
———. *Rationality and Irrationality in Economy*. Translated by Brian Pearce. New York: Monthly Review Press, 1974.
Goldmann, L. *Marxisme et sciences humaines*. Paris: Gallimard, 1971.
———. *Rechercher dialectique*. Paris: Gallimard, 1959.
Goux, J-J. *Economie et symbolique: Marx, Freud*. Paris: Seuil, 1973.
Gramsci, A. *Prison Notebooks*. Translated and edited by Quintin Hoare and Geoffrey Nowell Smith. New York: International Publishers, 1971.
———. *Selected Political Writings, 1910–1920*. Edited by Quintin Hoare and translated by John Mathers. New York: International Publishers, 1977.
Greimas, A. J. "Structure et histoire." *Les Temps Modernes* 246 (November 1966): 815–27.
Habermas, J. *Knowledge and Human Interests*. Translated by J. Shapiro. Boston: Beacon Press, 1971.
———. *Legitimation Crisis*. Translated by Thomas McCarthy. Boston: Beacon Press, 1975.
———. *Theory and Practice*. Translated by J. Shapiro. Boston: Beacon Press, 1974.
Hegel, G. W. F. *Phenomenology of Spirit*. Translated by A. V. Miller. London: Oxford University Press, 1977.
———. *Philosophy of History*. Translated by J. Sibree. New York: Dover, 1956.
Heller, A. *The Theory of Need in Marx*. Translated with introduction by Ken Coates and Stephen Bodington. New York: St. Martin's Press, 1976.
Horkheimer, M. *Critical Theory*. Translated by Mathew J. O'Connel and others. New York: Seabury Press, 1973.
Hyppolite, J. *Studies in Marx and Hegel*. Translated by John O'Neill. New York: Basic Books, 1969.
Iggers, G. *The German Conception of History*. Middletown: Wesleyan University Press, 1968.
———. *New Directions in European Historiography*. Middletown: Wesleyan University Press, 1975.
Jaeggi, U. J. V. *Ordung und Chaos: Der Strukturalismus als Methode und Mode*. Frankfurt am Main: Suhrkamp Verlag, 1968.
Jameson, F. *Marxism and Form*. Princeton: Princeton University Press, 1971.
Jay, M. *Dialectical Imagination: A History of the Frankfurt School and the Institute for Social Research, 1923–1950*. Boston: Little, Brown and Company, 1973.
Korsch, K. *Marxism and Philosophy*. Translated by Fred Halliday. New York: Modern Reader, 1970.
Kosik, K. *La Dialectique du concret*. Paris: Maspero, 1970.
Kristeva, J. *Recherches pour une sémanalyse*. Paris: Editions du Seuil, 1969.
Kuhn, T. *The Structure of Scientific Revolutions*. 2d ed. enlarged. Chicago: University of Chicago Press, 1970.
Lacan, J. *Ecrits*. Paris: Editions du Seuil, 1966.
———. *The Language of the Self: The Function of Language in Psychoanaly-*

sis. Translated with notes and commentary by Anthony Wilden. Baltimore: Johns Hopkins University Press, 1968.
Lakatos, I., and Musgrave, A., eds. *Criticism and the Growth of Knowledge*. Cambridge: Cambridge University Press, 1970.
Leach, E. *Claude Levi-Strauss*. New York: Viking Press, 1970.
Lecourt, D. *Epistemology and Marxism*. Translated by Ben Brewster. London: New Left Books, 1975.
Lefebvre, H. *Au-delà du structuralisme*. Paris: Anthropos, 1971.
Leiss, William. *The Limits to Satisfaction: The Problem of Needs and Commodities*. Toronto: University of Toronto Press, 1976.
Levi-Strauss, C. *Anthropologie structurale*. Paris: Plon, 1958.
———. *The Elementary Structures of Kinship*. Translated by Rodney Needham. Boston: Beacon Press, 1969.
———. *From Honey to Ashes*. Translated by John and Doreen Weightman. New York: Harper Torchbooks, 1973.
———. "Introduction à l'oeuvre de Marcel Mauss." In *Sociologie et anthropologie*, by M. Mauss. Paris: Presses Universitaires de France, 1950.
———. *L'Homme nu*. Paris: Plon, 1971.
———. *The Raw and the Cooked*. Translated by John and Doreen Weightman. New York: Harper Torchbooks, 1969.
———. *The Savage Mind*. Chicago: University of Chicago Press, 1968.
———. *Structural Anthropology*. Translated by Claire Jacobson and B. G. Schoepf. New York: Anchor Books, 1967.
———. *Structural Anthropology*. Vol. 2. Translated by Monique Layton. New York: Basic Books, 1977.
———. *Tristes tropiques*. Translated by John and Doreen Weightman. New York: Harper Torchbooks, 1974.
Lichtheim, G. *From Marx to Hegel*. New York: Herder and Herder, 1971.
———. *Marxism: A Historical and Critical Study*. New York: Praeger Publishers, 1965.
Lukacs, G. *History and Class Consciousness*. Translated by Rodney Livingstone. Cambridge: MIT Press, 1971.
———. *The Theory of the Novel*. Translated by Anna Bostock. Cambridge: MIT Press, 1971.
Macherey, P. *Pour une theorie de la production litteraire*. Paris: Maspero, 1967.
Macksey, R., and Donato, E., eds. *The Language of Criticism and the Sciences of Man: The Structuralist Controversy*. Baltimore: John Hopkins University Press, 1970.
Malinowski, B. *Argonauts of the Western Pacific*. New York: E. P. Dutton and Co., 1950.
Mandeville, B. *Fable of the Bees; or, Private Vices, Public Benefits*. Oxford: Clarendon Press, 1924.
Marcuse, H. *Eros and Civilization*. New York: Vintage Books, 1961.
———. *Five Lectures*. Boston: Beacon Press, 1969.
———. *Reason and Revolution: Hegel and the Rise of Social Theory*. Boston: Beacon Press, 1960.

Bibliography

Marx, K. *Capital.* Vol. 1. Translated by Ben Fowkes. London: Penguin Books, 1976.
———. *Capital.* Vol. 3. Edited by F. Engels. New York: International Publishers, 1972.
———. *A Contribution to the Critique of Political Economy.* Edited by Maurice Dobb. Translated by S. Ryazanskaya. New York: International Publishers, 1970.
———. *The Grundrisse: Introduction to the Critique of Political Economy.* Translated by Martin Nicolaus. London: Penguin Books, 1973.
———. *The Poverty of Philosophy.* New York: International Publishers, 1971.
Marx, K., and Engels, F. *Collected Works.* Vols. 1–9. New York: International Publishers, 1975.
Marx, K., and Engels, F. *The German Ideology.* Translated by S. Ryazanskaya. Moscow: Progress Publishers, 1968.
Mauss, Marcel. *See* Claude Levi-Strauss.
Merleau-Ponty, M. *Les Aventures de la dialectique.* Paris: Gallimard, 1955.
Meszaros, I. *Marx's Theory of Alienation.* London: Merlin Press, 1970.
Millet, L., and D'Ainville, M. V. *Le Structuralisme.* Paris: Editions Universitaires, 1970.
Paci, E. *The Function of Science and the Meaning of Man.* Translated by Paul Piccone and James E. Hansen. Evanston: Northwestern University Press, 1972.
Palmier, J. M. *Lacan: Le Symbolique et l'imaginaire.* Paris: Editions Universitaires, 1970.
Piaget, J. *Structuralism.* Translated and edited by Caninah Maschler. New York: Harper Torchbooks, 1970.
Popper, K. *Conjectures and Refutations.* New York: Harper and Row, 1963.
———. *The Open Society and Its Enemies.* Vols. 1 and 2. Princeton: Princeton University Press, 1966.
———. *The Poverty of Historicism.* Boston: Beacon Press, 1957.
Ranciere, J., et al. *Lire Le Capital.* Vol. 2. Paris: Maspero, 1965.
———. "Mode d'emploi pur une réédition de *Lire le Capital.*" *Les Temps Modernes* 328 (November 1973): 788–807.
———. "Sur la théorie de l'idéologie politique d'Althusser." *L'Homme et la société* 27 (January–February–March 1973): 31–61.
Ricoeur, P. *Freud and Philosophy: An Essay on Interpretation.* Translated by Denis Savage. New Haven: Yale University Press, 1970.
Robey, D., ed. *Structuralism: An Introduction.* London: Oxford University Press, 1972.
Rossi, I., ed. *The Unconscious in Culture: The Structuralism of Claude Levi-Strauss in Perspective.* New York: Dutton, 1974.
Sahlins, Marshall. *Culture and Practical Reason.* Chicago: University of Chicago Press, 1976.
Sartre, J-P. *Critique de la raison dialectique: Théorie des ensembles practiques.* Vol. 1. Paris: Gallimard, 1960.
Schiwy, G. *Strukturalismus und Zeichensysteme.* Munich: C. H. Beck Verlag, 1973.

Schmidt, A., ed. *Beiträge zur marxistischen Erkenntnistheorie.* Frankfurt am Main: Suhrkamp, 1969.
———. *The Concept of Nature in Marx.* Translated by Ben Fowkes. London: New Left Books, 1971.
———. *Geschichte und Struktur: Fragen einer marxistischen Historik.* Munich: Reiche Hanser, 1971.
Schneider, M., *Neurosis and Civilization: A Marxist/Freudian Synthesis.* Translated by Michael Roloff. New York: Seabury Press, 1975.
Sebag, L. *Marxisme et structuralisme.* Paris: Payot, 1964.
Simonis, Y. *Claude Levi-Strauss ou la passion de l'inceste.* Paris: Aubier-Montaigne, 1968.
Smith, Adam. *The Wealth of Nations.* New York: The Modern Library, 1965.
Sollers, P., et al. *Théorie d'ensemble: Collection tel quel.* Paris: Seuil, 1968.
Steiner, George. *After Babel.* New York: Oxford University Press, 1975.
Timpanaro, S. *On Materialism.* Translated by Lawrence Garner. London: New Left Books, 1975.
Verstaeten, P. "Levi-Strauss ou la tentation de néant." *Les Temps Modernes* 206–8 (1963):66–109, 507–52.
Vico, G. *The New Science.* Translated by Thomas G. Bergin and with introduction by Max Fisch. Ithaca: Cornell University Press, 1970.
Weber, M. *The Protestant Ethic and the Spirit of Capitalism.* New York: Scribner, 1960.
Wellmer, A. *Critical Theory of Society.* Translated by John Cumming. New York: Herder and Herder, 1971.
Williams, R. *Keywords: A Vocabulary of Culture and Society.* New York: Oxford University Press, 1976.
———. *Marxism and Literature.* New York: Oxford University Press, 1977.

Index

Adorno, T. W., 75–77
Alienation, 63, 70, 83. *See also* Objectification
Arendt, Hannah, 18, 79–87, 92
Aristotle, 79–80

Baudrillard, Jean, 18, 44–57, 58, 59, 72–74, 79, 83, 86, 87

Code, 64–68
Commodity-form, 25–33, 47, 49, 53, 67, 69, 72, 78, 87
Consumption, 47, 54, 79
Culture. *See* Objectification; Superstructure

Deleuze, Gilles, 18, 58–74, 79, 83, 93
Desire, 58–74. *See also* Oedipus complex
Dialectical logic, 34–35, 37, 50

Economic determinism, 1–3, 9–15, 30, 33, 36, 55, 69, 79

Feuerbach, Ludwig, 23
Foucault, Michel, 54, 95–96n
Freud, Sigmund, 37–42, 61–63, 93

Galileo, 16
Goux, Jean-Joseph, 30–44, 46, 58, 88, 92, 93
Gramsci, Antonio, 76–77
Guattari, Felix, 18, 58–74, 79, 83, 93

Habermas, Jurgen, 18, 79, 84–86, 88
Harris, Marvin, 18
Hegel, G.W.F., 3–7, 26, 34, 44, 50, 51, 66, 87, 92
Hobbes, Thomas, 93
Homo economicus, 23, 44, 87

Ideology, 15, 23, 47, 58, 73, 75–78, 81, 87, 88

Labor, 2–10, 25. *See also* Objectification
Lakatos, Imre, 89–91
Levi-Strauss, Claude, 18–20, 22–25, 31, 35, 42, 44–45, 52, 63, 92
Lukacs, Georg, 91–92

Malinowski, Bronislaw, 35–36, 53
Mandeville, Bernard, 2
Marx, Karl, works of:
 Capital, 1, 8, 9, 18, 25–30, 33, 36, 39, 46, 48–50, 51, 78, 82, 88

Communist Manifesto, 55, 78
Contribution to a Critique of Political Economy, 11, 26, 66
Economic and Philosophic Manuscripts, 1–4, 8, 70, 73
German Ideology, 7–8, 12, 23, 77–79
The Grundrisse, 1, 12, 24, 30, 49, 51, 59
Mauss, Marcel, 52
Morgan, Lewis Henry, 17

Nietzsche, Friedrich, 93

Objectification, 3, 5–11, 14, 75, 84
Oedipus complex, 61–62, 71–72

Popper, Karl, 89–91
Praxis (practice), 14, 23, 50, 85
Psychoanalysis, 61–62, 71. *See also* Freud
Purposive activity, 8, 23. *See also* Labor; Objectification
Putnam, Hilary, 90

Schizophrenia, 60, 61, 62, 70, 71
Science, 89–91, 93
Semiology, 30–43, 45–46, 48
Sahlins, Marshall, 18, 86
Smith, Adam, 1–2
Species-being, 4, 23
Steiner, George, 95n
Structuralism, 19–25, 40–43. *See also* Semiology
Superstructure (infrastructure), 1, 11, 12, 16–18, 23, 31, 44, 47, 50, 63, 73, 74, 76–79, 81, 85, 86, 88, 89
Symbolic exchange, 18, 19, 20–24, 30–43, 45, 47, 52–54, 74, 79, 85, 93

Use value, 47–52
Utilitarianism, 2, 7, 25, 36, 46, 48, 49, 51, 53, 54, 57, 74, 80–86

Vico, Giambattista, 5

Weber, Max, 28, 33
Williams, Raymond, 88

UNIVERSITY OF FLORIDA MONOGRAPHS

Humanities

No. 1: *Uncollected Letters of James Gates Percival*, edited by Harry R. Warfel

No. 2: *Leigh Hunt's Autobiography: The Earliest Sketches*, edited by Stephen F. Fogle

No. 3: *Pause Patterns in Elizabethan and Jacobean Drama*, by Ants Oras

No. 4: *Rhetoric and American Poetry of the Early National Period*, by Gordon E. Bigelow

No. 5: *The Background of* The Princess Casamassima, by W. H. Tilley

No. 6: *Indian Sculpture in the John and Mable Ringling Museum of Art*, by Roy C. Craven, Jr.

No. 7: *The Cestus. A Mask*, edited by Thomas B. Stroup

No. 8: Tamburlaine, Part I, *and Its Audience*, by Frank B. Fieler

No. 9: *The Case of John Darrell: Minister and Exorcist*, by Corinne Holt Rickert

No. 10: *Reflections of the Civil War in Southern Humor*, by Wade H. Hall

No. 11: *Charles Dodgson, Semeiotician*, by Daniel F. Kirk

No. 12: *Three Middle English Religious Poems*, edited by R. H. Bowers

No. 13: *The Existentialism of Miguel de Unamuno*, by José Huertas-Jourda

No. 14: *Four Spiritual Crises in Mid-Century American Fiction*, by Robert Detweiler

No. 15: *Style and Society in German Literary Expressionism*, by Egbert Krispyn

No. 16: *The Reach of Art: A Study in the Prosody of Pope*, by Jacob H. Adler

No. 17: *Malraux, Sartre, and Aragon as Political Novelists*, by Catherine Savage

No. 18: *Las Guerras Carlistas y el Reinado Isabelino en la Obra de Ramón del Valle-Inclán*, por María Dolores Lado

No. 19: *Diderot's* Vie de Sénèque: *A Swan Song Revised*, by Douglas A. Bonneville

No. 20: *Blank Verse and Chronology in Milton*, by Ants Oras

No. 21: *Milton's Elisions*, by Robert O. Evans

No. 22: *Prayer in Sixteenth-Century England*, by Faye L. Kelly

No. 23: *The Strangers: The Tragic World of Tristan L'Hermite*, by Claude K. Abraham

No. 24: *Dramatic Uses of Biblical Allusion in Marlowe and Shakespeare*, by James H. Sims

No. 25: *Doubt and Dogma in Maria Edgeworth*, by Mark D. Hawthorne

No. 26: *The Masses of Francesco Soriano*, by Philip Kniseley

No. 27: *Love as Death in* The Iceman Cometh, by Winifred Dusenbury Frazer

No. 28: *Melville and Authority*, by Nicholas Canaday, Jr.

No. 29: *Don Quixote: Hero or Fool? A Study in Narrative Technique*, by John J. Allen

No. 30: *Ideal and Reality in the Fictional Narratives of Théophile Gautier*, by Albert B. Smith

No. 31: *Negritude as a Theme in the Poetry of the Portuguese-Speaking World*, by Richard A. Preto-Rodas

No. 32: *The Criticism of Photography as Art: The Photographs of Jerry Uelsmann*, by John L. Ward

No. 33: *The Kingdom of God in the Synoptic Tradition*, by Richard H. Hiers

No. 34: *Dante Gabriel Rossetti's Versecraft*, by Joseph F. Vogel

No. 35: *T. S. Eliot's Concept of Language: A Study of Its Development*, by Harry T. Antrim

No. 36: *The Consolatio Genre in Medieval English Literature*, by Michael H. Means

No. 37: *Melville's Angles of Vision*, by A. Carl Bredahl, Jr.

No. 38: *The Historical Jesus and the Kingdom of God*, by Richard H. Hiers

No. 39: *In Adam's Garden: A Study of John Clare's Pre-Asylum Poetry*, by Janet M. Todd

No. 40: *Democracy, Stoicism, and Education: An Essay in the History of Freedom and Reason*, by Robert R. Sherman

No. 41: *On Defining the Proper Name*, by John Algeo

No. 42: *The Henley-Stevenson Quarrel*, by Edward H. Cohen

No. 43: *E.G. and E.G.O.: Emma Goldman and* The Iceman Cometh, by Winifred L. Frazer

No. 44: *The Mexican Cult of Death in Myth and Literature*, by Barbara L. C. Brodman

No. 45: *The Legend of Herostratus: Existential Envy in Rousseau and Unamuno*, by Gregory L. Ulmer

No. 46: *Don Quixote: Hero or Fool?* Part II, by John J. Allen

No. 47: *Soviet Satire of the Twenties*, by Richard L. Chapple

No. 48: *Collaboration et originalité chez La Rochefoucauld*, by Susan Read Baker

No. 49: *"The Unsearchable Wisdom of God": A Study of Providence in Richardson's* Pamela, by James Louis Fortuna, Jr.

No. 50: *Marx and Philosophy of Culture*, by Robert D'Amico